# In the Kitchen with Grandma

# In the Kitchen with Grandma

## INEZ FERRARI

SIXTH&SPRING BOOKS

NEW YORK

Editorial Director
Trisha Malcolm

Art Director
Christy Hale

Copy Editor
Jonna Gallo

Illustrations
Christy Hale

Managers, Book Division
Shannon Kerner
Michelle Lo

Production Manager
David Joinnides

President and Publisher, Sixth&Spring Books
Art Joinnides

Copyright © 1994 by Inez Ferrari
Library of Congress Cataloging-in-Publication Data
Ferrari, Inez.
In the kitchen with Grandma / Inez Ferrari.
p. cm.
ISBN 1-931543-70-4
1. Cookery. I. Title.

TX714.F468 2004
641.5–dc22                                    2004051771

For my mother and father and my husband Rudy, whose love of good home cooking was and is so much a part of life and whose encouragement instilled an appreciation of *"buona cucina."* This book would not have come to be if not for my five wonderful daughters (Leslie, Gigi, Gabrielle, Mimi, Niki) who kept insisting that I record their favorite family recipes. Very special thanks to Gigi for spending many precious hours typing and deciphering my scribbles.

# Contents

## Meats & Fish 83

## Desserts 107

## CHRISTMAS DELIGHTS

## LITTLE NONNA'S HOLIDAY RECIPES

# Index

# Introduction

This cookbook was a labor of love for my five wonderful daughters: Leslie, Gigi, Gabrielle, Michelle and Nicole. For years they've called me for one recipe or another. Realizing that some family recipes could be lost forever, I finally decided to gather them, and other favorites, together in a small, modest cookbook for my girls and my grandchildren.

I come from a warm, loving family whose great joy was to entertain relatives and friends. Of course, along with that went good food and drink and singing old Italian songs at the end of the meal.

I grew up with a love for cooking and good food. The first thing I ever made was pineapple upside-down cake for my father. It must have been less than terrific but my father thought it was the best he ever had (or so he said). I can still remember coming home from school to the aroma of freshly baked bread or padelletti (pancakes Italian style). Mama (Little Nonna) always made her soup from scratch. She'd send me to the butcher up the street for short ribs or soup chicken and she'd call after me, "Don't forget to ask him for the knuckle bones!" We'd have calf liver, smothered in onions and red wine, once a week ("because it makes the blood strong"); boiled beef (from the soup) and vegetables with a green vinaigrette sauce; and chicken in every way imaginable.

My father never went hunting, but my husband's father (Nonno Joe) did. Occasionally, in the fall, we'd have polenta with rabbit or polenta with sausage or stew. Baccalà (salted cod) was traditionally served on New Year's Day, as were lentils with cotecchino (a large sausage) for good luck in the year to come. Veal was another meat prepared in many ways (stuffed, in stew, rolled, sautéed!). Of course, every special occasion called for ravioli or anolini. Risotto, gnocchi and torte were for everyday meals.

All in all, I've always felt that our casalinga (homestyle) Italian cooking has always been comfort food with earthy, warm, colorful and honest flavors—in short, happy food!

It's up to you to remember and pass along this feeling to your families. Innovate, add your own recipes, improve on mine, that's what it's all about. Learn from what you are exposed to and most of all enjoy the whole process. Cook with love; Little Nonna did and so do I. It does make a difference.

I've interspersed a few special poems that express my feelings at different times of my life. In this way, you'll understand me better. Add your own special moments and recipes. I love you all very much. *Tanto, tanto, tanto!*

# Abbreviations & Conversion Tables

| | | |
|---|---|---|
| t = teaspoon | pkg = package | 2T = 1 fluid oz |
| T = tablespoon | sm = small | 8T = ½ C or 4 oz |
| oz = ounce | med = medium | 16T = 1 C or 8 oz |
| C = cup | lg = large | ¼ C = 4T |
| pt = pint | pinch or few grains | ⅓ C = 5T |
| qt = quart | = less than ⅛ t | 2C = 1 pt or 16 oz |
| gal = gallon | 72 drops = 1t | 1 qt = 2 pt or 4 C |
| lb = pound | 3t = 1T | 1 gal = 4 qt |

# Tips Worth Remembering

1. Fresh lemon juice will remove the lingering scent of onion from your hands.

2. When hands are badly soiled, put 1t sugar in one of your palms before lathering up with soap; the granules gently scrub away grime.

3. Clean darkened aluminum pans by boiling in them 2t cream of tartar and 1 qt water for 10 minutes.

4. Plant dill near tomato plants to prevent tomato worms.

5. To discourage rodents from prowling your vegetable beds, plant marigolds nearby.

6. Boil a cracked dish for 45 minutes in sweet milk and the crack will weld together.

7. When poaching eggs, add 1T of white vinegar to water to help set the whites. Also add it to water when boiling eggs to neatly seal any cracks that occur.

8. To prevent freshly-cut fruit, such as bananas, apples or pears, from darkening, spritz them with lemon juice.

9. Keep in mind that when and how you add salt does matter. In soups and sauces, add it early; for meat dishes, add just before removing from the stove. For vegetables, add it to cooking water; for fish, put it in the pan when frying.

10. To absorb the strong odor of cabbage, place a small cup of vinegar near the stove.

11. To remove ball point pen stains from clothes, rub lightly with petroleum jelly before laundering.

# Mini Menus

**1**

Mom's Pot Roast
Sweet and Sour Cabbage
Cornbread
Apple Pie

**2**

Mom's Pot Roast
Noodles
Chocolate Chip Cake

**3**

Ravioli and Tomato Sauce
with Meatballs
Mixed Salad
Foccaccia

**4**

Corned Beef with Boiled
Potatoes, Cabbage, Carrots
and Onions
Mustard/Horseradish Sauce
Irish Soda Bread
Beer
Chocolate Mocha Graham
Cracker Pie

## 5

Poached Salmon
Risotto with Peas
Fruit Salad

## 6

Polenta with Tomato Sauce
Bolognese
Mixed Salad
Ricotta Pudding

## 7

Risotto with Meat and
Mushroom Sauce
Mixed Salad
Baked Caramel Custard

## 8

Minestrone
Mozzarella in Carozza
(Melted Cheese on
Italian Bread)
Nonna's Cherry Tart

## 9

Uccelletti
Stuffed Onions
Mushrooms Trifolati
Mom's Fabulous
Cheesecake

"I love you, Johnny," said mother one day,
"I love you more than I can say."
Then she answered his questions with,
"Don't bother me now!"
And she didn't have time to show him how
to hook up his tractor to his plow.

But she washed the windows and scrubbed the floor
and baked and cooked and cleaned some more.
"Bring Bobby in? Well I should say not! You'd track
my floor and I don't want a spot."

"No, we haven't time for a story today, I'm cooking
for company, so run out and play."
"Maybe tomorrow," she said with a sigh. And
Johnny went out, almost ready to cry.

"I love you, Johnny," again she said as she washed
his face and sent him to bed.
Now how do you think that Johnny guessed if it was
him or the house that she loved best?

Anonymous

Get the message? Make time for your
children—they grow up too fast.

# Appetizers & Party Foods

# Sandwich Party Loaf

## Ingredients

4 hard-cooked eggs
2 celery stalks, chopped
5T mayonnaise
1 carrot, grated
1 can deviled ham
1T pickle relish
1T mustard
1 can chicken spread
1 pimento, chopped
parsley and desired herbs
butter
1 loaf of white bread, sliced horizontally in layers, crust removed
1 8-oz pkg cream cheese
2T cream or milk

## Servings : 12

I used to make this for luncheon parties.
I also made it for Nicole's baby shower. It's always a hit!

❶ Combine eggs, 1 stalk celery, carrot, 3T mayo and desired herbs into egg salad.

❷ Combine deviled ham, pickle relish, mustard and desired herbs in separate bowl.

❸ Combine chicken spread, 2T mayo, pimento, parsley and desired herbs in separate bowl.

❹ Take bottom layer of bread; lightly butter one side. Place on party platter with small pieces of waxed paper underneath to keep platter clean. Cover with a thin layer of egg salad.

❺ Take the next layer of bread; lightly butter both sides. Place it on top of the bottom layer. Cover with a thin layer of deviled ham spread.

❻ Take the third layer of bread; lightly butter both sides. Place it on top of the previous layer. Cover with a thin layer of chicken spread.

❼ Continue in this manner until you get to the top piece of bread. This is only buttered on its downward-facing side and gets no butter on top.

❽ Place cream cheese and milk in a separate bowl; whip until soft and smooth.

❾ Frost entire loaf with cream cheese frosting. Garnish as desired. Remove waxed paper. Chill; slice; serve.

# Seafood Fancy

❶ Combine all ingredients in bowl. Put into a casserole dish; top with crumbs. Bake at 350°F for 45-50 minutes or until golden brown. Serve with pumpernickel rounds.

My friend Jonna Sue gave me this, it's a good do-ahead recipe.

## Ingredients
1 can crab
1 C shrimp
1 C chopped celery
$^1/_2$ C chopped pepper
1 C mayonnaise
1$^1/_2$ t Worcestershire sauce
$^1/_2$ t salt
pepper

## BUTTER CRUMBS
1 C bread crumbs
+
2 T melted butter

## Servings : 6

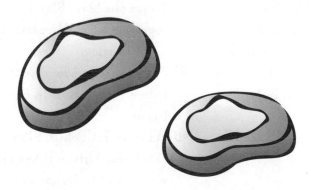

# Cheese Puffs

## Ingredients

¹/₄ lb grated American
or Cheddar cheese

¹/₄ C butter

¹/₂ C flour

¹/₈ t salt

Servings : 2¹/₂ dozen

❶ Place all ingredients in a bowl. Blend until smooth.

❷ Refrigerate 30 minutes. With your hands, form into ¹/₂" balls. Return to refrigerator.

❸ Twenty minutes before serving, heat oven to 350°F. Bake for 10 to 15 minutes. Serve immediately.


# Three Cheese Nut Roll

## Ingredients

¹/₃ C crumbled blue cheese

1 3-oz cream cheese

1¹/₂ C sharp Cheddar

¹/₂ t Worcestershire sauce

chopped nuts

Servings : 8 to 10

❶ Bring cheese to room temperature. Grate cheddar. Blend all cheeses together with Worcestershire sauce until creamy.

❷ Put onto wax paper; with hands, form into a 7" log. Roll in chopped nuts to coat.

❸ Wrap in foil; chill. Slice; serve with crackers. This will keep for several weeks and is delicious with fruit and raisins.

When I was a young bride, we entertained a lot. This was an easy do-ahead recipe that I served with drinks.

# Cheese/Clam Dip

❶ Beat cream cheese until light and fluffy; add clam juice and drained clams. Blend.

❷ Add all other ingredients; blend. Chill. Serve with crackers.

## Ingredients

$^1/_2$ lb cream cheese

2 T clam juice

1 10$^1/_2$-oz can minced clams

Pinch onion and garlic salt

1t Worcestershire sauce

1t chopped celery

### Servings : 8 to 10

# Miracle Mushrooms

### Ingredients

1 lb sliced mushrooms

1 C heavy cream

$^1/_2$ t salt

pepper

1 T lemon juice

---

### Servings : 4

❶ Place mushrooms in large skillet; add cream, salt, pepper and lemon juice.

❷ Cook on Low heat for 20 minutes, stirring occasionally, to thicken into a delicious spread. Serve with melba toast.

# Party Dip for Raw Vegetables

### Ingredients

$^1/_2$ sm carrot

$^1/_2$ onion

$^1/_4$ green pepper

parsley

$^1/_2$ C Ricotta Cheese

1 C mayonnaise

$^1/_4$ t salt

pepper

2 T vinegar

---

### Servings : 8 to 10

❶ Chop all vegetables very fine. Combine with remaining ingredients; blend well. Chill. Serve as a dip for chilled veggies.

# Play Dough

❶ Combine cornstarch and $\frac{1}{2}$C cold water in a large bowl. Mix.

❷ Combine salt and $\frac{2}{3}$C lukewarm water in saucepan. Mix over Low heat until hot.

❸ Stir in cornstarch mixture; cook approximately 5 minutes.

❹ Pour onto table and knead. Separate into balls; tint with coloring.

❺ Have hours of rainy-day fun!

## Ingredients

1C cornstarch
$\frac{1}{2}$C cold water
2C salt
$\frac{2}{3}$C lukewarm water
food coloring

---

**Servings :** Don't be silly. Let's have fun!!!

Monday's child is fair of face,
Tuesday's child is full of grace,
Wednesday's child is full of woe,
Thursday's child has far to go,
Friday's child is loving and giving,
Saturday's child works hard for a living,
But the child that's born on the Sabbath day
is fair and wise and good and gay.

Anonymous

# Leek and Potato Soup

## Ingredients

2–3 leeks, washed and
finely-chopped
4T butter
1 lg can chicken broth
2 potatoes, diced
$\frac{1}{2}$C heavy cream

### Servings : 6 to 8

❶ Sauté leeks in butter.
❷ Add broth and potatoes; bring to boil.
❸ Simmer until potatoes are cooked through.
❹ Take off heat; whirl in blender or push through a strainer to achieve desired consistency.
❺ Stir in heavy cream; let cool. Can be served warm or chilled.

Note: This soup can be frozen if desired. To do so, stop after Step 4; soup should not be frozen with cream. Instead, add cream when reheating.

# Stracciatella (Italian Egg Drop Soup)

## Ingredients

2–3C chicken broth
2 eggs
$\frac{1}{2}$C Parmesan cheese
pinch salt and pepper

### Servings : 2 to 3

❶ Bring broth to boil.
❷ Beat eggs, cheese, salt and pepper together in small bowl.
❸ Add egg and cheese mixture slowly to boiling broth and whisk with a fork until little pieces are formed (Stracciatella means "little rags"). Serve.

My mom would often make this when one of us didn't feel well. It's light yet comforting and nourishing. Try it next time someone has a cold.

# Onion Soup

1. Combine oil and butter in heavy saucepan; heat.
2. Add onions, cover; sauté slowly for 12 minutes.
3. Uncover; cook slowly until dark brown.
4. Add garlic, salt, pepper.
5. Sprinkle in flour; stir. Add wine; simmer for 3 minutes.
6. Add boiling broth; cook slowly for 10 minutes.
7. Ladle soup into individual crocks. Cover surface with toasted bread and cheese. Broil briefly to melt cheese. Serve.

I love onion soup. Sometimes I put Muenster cheese on the toasted bread, then sprinkle with grated cheese. Delicious!

## Ingredients

2T olive oil

3T butter

4C thinly-sliced onions

1 garlic clove (optional)

1t salt

1t pepper

$1\frac{1}{2}$T flour

1C red wine

8C beef broth, boiling

6–8 pieces Italian bread, toasted

$1\frac{1}{2}$C Parmesan cheese

### Servings : 6 to 8

# Minestrone

## Ingredients

1 onion, chopped

3T each oil and butter

2 celery stalks, chopped

3 carrots, diced

½ head cabbage/escarole, chopped

2 tomatoes, peeled

2C water

4 potatoes, cubed

½C canned kidney beans

½ pkg dried split peas

1t salt

pinch pepper

2C broth

2 bouillon cubes

¼C rice or macaroni

Parmesan cheese

## Servings : 6

❶ Fry chopped onion in 3T butter and oil. Add celery, carrots, cabbage or escarole.

❷ Add tomatoes; fry until water evaporates, approximately 10 minutes. Add water; cover.

❸ Add potatoes, beans, split peas, salt and pepper. Boil uncovered for 1 hour.

❹ Add more broth or water if necessary.

❺ Add bouillon cubes.

❻ Simmer, covered, for 1 hour.

❼ Add rice or macaroni if desired; keep on heat briefly to cook through.

For best results, dried beans should be soaked in warm water overnight.

This delicious, nutritious soup, is a wintertime favorite with the men in my family. This soup can be pureed, and it can also be frozen or refrigerated for up to 1 week. Meat or ham bones can add extra flavor. Add grated Parmesan cheese on top of each serving.

Rudy's version includes: 8 qts water; salt; pepper; garlic salt; large Savoy cabbage, shredded; 1 small head escarole, chopped; celery tops; 3 carrots, chopped; leek tops, chopped; 1–2 onions, chopped; 1 lb potatoes, chopped; $^1/_2$C dried beans; $1^1/_2$ lb string beans; 1 large can peeled tomatoes; $^1/_2$C olive oil; $^1/_2$ lb butter and 2C cooked rice. THIS IS WONDERFUL and yields 5 quarts of soup, some of which can be frozen for another day.

This is what Italians call a "ciapa chi ciapa" soup. In other words, improvise your own version with whatever ingredients you have on hand.

# Cream of Broccoli or Zucchini Soup

## Ingredients

3–4 large broccoli
or zucchini
4T butter
1 onion, finely chopped
1 lg can chicken broth
4T heavy cream

## Servings: 1½ quarts

❶ Wash broccoli or wash, split and remove seeds from zucchini. Chop.

❷ Melt butter in pan; add onions. Cook 5 minutes or until soft but not browned.

❸ Add broccoli or zucchini; sprinkle with black pepper. Add broth; cook 1 hour or until zucchini or broccoli is soft.

❹ Puree soup in blender. You may need to work in batches.

❺ Return to pan, bring to a boil. Stir in cream; serve immediately.

This is an easy and refreshing soup—one of Rudy's favorites, especially when his garden overflowed with zucchini. To freeze, proceed through step 4, then allow to cool. Stir in cream when reheating.

# Black Bean Soup

❶ Wash and pick over beans; cover in water and soak overnight. The next morning, add water to make 6 cups of liquid and place in a large pot.

❷ Cook onion, green pepper and garlic in olive oil for 5 minutes; add to beans. Add bone, seasonings and bacon. Cover; simmer 2 to 3 hours or until beans begin to fall apart, adding more water if necessary.

❸ Add wine vinegar. Serve with a mound of rice; garnish each serving with a slice of lemon and onion, hard-cooked egg and a sprig of fresh parsley.

## Ingredients

1 lb dried black beans

water

1C chopped onion

1 green pepper, chopped

1 clove garlic, minced

$\frac{1}{2}$C olive oil

1 ham bone

2 bay leaves + parsley sprigs

2t salt

$\frac{1}{4}$t pepper

1 slice bacon, minced

$\frac{1}{4}$C wine vinegar

Hot cooked rice

lemon slices

1 chopped, hard-cooked egg

onion slices

## Servings : 3 quarts

# New England Clam Chowder

## Ingredients

1 stalk celery, chopped

1 onion, chopped

2–3T butter or margarine

3 small cans chicken or
clam broth

1–2 potatoes, diced

2–3 cans minced clams

$\frac{1}{2}$C heavy cream

### Servings : 4

❶ Sauté celery and onion in butter until golden.

❷ Add broth and juice from canned clams.

❸ Add diced potatoes; cover and heat until potatoes are cooked through.

❹ Add minced clams; heat.

❺ Add cream; don't boil. Serve with saltines.

Using canned clams and canned broth means this chowder comes together very quickly and easily, and it's delicious.

# Shrimp Bisque

❶ Shell shrimp; cut into small pieces.
❷ Put tomatoes, stock, vegetables,
   seasonings and rice in kettle; bring
   to a boil. Cover; simmer for 1 hour.
❸ Force mixture through a fine sieve,
   or whirl smooth in an electric blender.
   Just before serving, add shrimp; heat.
❹ Heat cream; add to mixture. Season to
   taste. Serve at once with sherry and
   croutons. Garnish with lemon and
   chopped parsley.

### Ingredients

1½lbs cooked shrimp
2 19-oz cans tomatoes
2C beef stock or bouillon
2 sm onions, sliced
1C chopped celery
2 small carrots, sliced
2 sprigs parsley
6 whole black peppers
1 sm bay leaf
pinch of thyme
3t salt
3T rice
1 pint light cream
sherry
croutons
thin slices of lemon
parsley, chopped

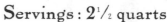

### Servings : 2½ quarts

# All I Really Need to Know
# I Learned in Kindergarten

Most of what I really need to know
about how to live and what to do and how to be
I learned in kindergarten. Wisdom was
not at the top of the graduate school mountain,
but there in the sandpile at Sunday School.
These are the things I learned:

Share everything.
Play fair.
Don't hit people.
Put things back where you found them.
Clean up your own mess.
Don't take things that aren't yours.
Say you're sorry when you hurt somebody.
Wash your hands before you eat.
Flush.
Warm cookies and cold milk are good for you.
Live a balanced life—learn some and think some
and draw and paint and sing and dance
and play and work every day some.
Take a nap every afternoon.
When you go out into the world, watch out for
traffic, hold hands, and stick together.
Be aware of wonder.

Robert Fulghum

# Breads
## & Breakfast Treats

# Corn Bread

## Ingredients

1 C flour

$^3/_4$ C yellow cornmeal

$^3/_4$ C sugar

1 t salt

3$^1/_2$ t baking powder

2 eggs

1 C milk

2 T melted butter or margarine

## Servings : 1 loaf

❶ Sift flour, cornmeal, sugar, salt and baking powder twice.

❷ Beat eggs. Add milk and melted butter; beat well.

❸ Add blended liquids to dry ingredients; beat thoroughly.

❹ Pour into well-greased pan.

❺ Bake at 425°F for 25 minutes.

# Perfect Popovers

❶ Preheat oven to 400°F. This is critical
for popovers to rise properly.

❷ Whirl all ingredients in a blender
until smooth.

❸ Pour into greased muffin pan.

❹ Bake for 50 minutes. They should be
nicely browned and raised above the
edges of the muffin cups.

Popovers are raised only by steam and then
dropped into clumsy, delicious shapes.

## Ingredients
1 C milk

2 eggs

1 C flour

¼ t salt

---

### Servings : 8 popovers

# Muffins

## Ingredients

¹/₂ C butter

1 C sugar

2 eggs

2 C flour

2 t baking powder

¹/₂ t salt

1 t vanilla

¹/₂ C milk

2 C blueberries (optional)

2 T sugar with
¹/₄ t cinnamon

---

## Servings : 12 to 14 muffins

❶ Cream butter and sugar until fluffy.

❷ Add eggs; blend well.

❸ Sift dry ingredients together. Add half to butter-sugar-egg mixture; stir. Add milk and vanilla; stir. Add remaining dry ingredients; stir.

❹ If using, add blueberries; stir. Spoon batter into greased muffin pan. Sprinkle tops with cinnamon sugar.

❺ To make jam-filled treats, fill greased muffin cups partially with batter, place a spoonful of fruit preserves on top, then cover jam with more batter.

❻ Bake at 375°F for 25 minutes or until tester comes out clean.

Rudy would take a package of muffins into the office for breakfast. These freeze beautifully.

# Irish Soda Bread

❶ In large bowl, sift flour, salt, baking soda, baking powder and sugar.

❷ Cut in butter and mix until you have pea-sized pieces.

❸ In another bowl, beat egg and buttermilk (both should be brought to room temperature first).

❹ Pour liquids into dry ingredients; stir until well-blended. Add raisins; blend.

❺ Turn out onto floured board and knead until dough is smooth, approximately 3 minutes.

❻ Divide dough into two equal pieces. Shape into rounds and place in greased cake pans.

❼ Press to fill pans. With knife, cut a cross in top of each to allow steam to escape while baking.

❽ Bake at 375°F for 40 minutes.

❾ Turn out to cool. Let sit for 4 hours before cutting.

I make this and cornbread on St. Patty's Day. With butter, it's a nice breakfast bread anytime. Big Nonna made Ciambella, which is similar but dryer.

## Ingredients

4C flour

3T baking powder

1t salt

1t baking soda

¼C sugar

¼C (½ stick) butter

1 egg

1¾C buttermilk

1–2C raisins

## Servings : 2 loaves

# Cranberry Nut Loaf

## Ingredients

2 C flour

1 C sugar

1½ t baking powder

½ t baking soda

1 t salt

¼ C butter or margarine

1 room-temperature egg, beaten

¾ C orange juice

½ C nuts

1 C cranberries, halved

## Servings: 2 loaves

❶ In large bowl, sift flour, sugar, baking powder, baking soda and salt.

❷ In a food processor, or with a pastry blender, cut in butter until mix resembles coarse cornmeal.

❸ Combine beaten egg and juice in another bowl. Add liquid to dry ingredients. Mix just until damp, do not beat!

❹ Fold in chopped nuts and cranberries.

❺ Grease 2 loaf pans. Line pans with waxed paper; grease again.

❻ Divide batter evenly among pans. Push batter into corners; smooth tops. Let batters rest 20 minutes while oven preheats to 350°F.

❼ Bake 1 hour or until testers come out clean.

❽ Turn out onto racks. Peel off wax paper carefully.

❾ Allow loaves to sit overnight before slicing. Or, once cooled, wrap well and freeze for later.

We used to buy cranberries when we went to Cape Cod in the fall and use them for this recipe during the holidays. We'd freeze some loaves and give them out as Christmas gifts. It's also very nutritious—lots of vitamin C!

# Banana Bread

❶ Combine all dry ingredients in large bowl.

❷ Blend butter and sugar; beat in eggs and bananas.

❸ Stir into dry ingredients until blended.

❹ Grease loaf pan; pour into pan. Bake 45–50 minutes at 350°F.

### Ingredients

1³/₄C flour

³/₄t baking soda

¹/₂t salt

1¹/₄t cream of tartar

¹/₂C soft butter

³/₄C sugar

2 eggs

2 sm, ripe bananas

Servings : 1 loaf

# Applesauce Bread

❶ Cream butter and sugar; blend until light. Beat in egg; blend well.

❷ Sift together dry ingredients; add to creamed mixture; blend.

❸ Add raisins, nuts and applesauce; blend.

❹ Grease a loaf pan; pour batter into pan. Bake at 350°F for 50–60 minutes.

These last two breads are good keepers. Tasty on their own plain, they make delicious sandwiches when spread with cream cheese.

### Ingredients

¹/₂C butter or margarine

1C brown sugar

1 egg

1³/₄C flour

¹/₂t salt

1t baking soda

1t cinnamon

¹/₄t cloves (optional)

1C raisins

1C nuts (optional)

1C applesauce

Servings :1 loaf

# Buttermilk Pancakes

## Ingredients

1 C buttermilk
1 C flour
1 egg
1 t baking soda
$^1/_2$ t salt
1 T sugar (optional)
2 T melted butter (optional)

## Servings : 8 pancakes

❶ Put all ingredients into blender; whirl until smooth.

❷ Preheat griddle (grease if not non-stick). It is hot enough when a few drops of water sprinkled on it bead up and evaporate.

❸ Pour some batter onto griddle; cook until bubbles form and pop. Flip pancakes and brown other side.

Not only are these easy to make, but they are also more tender than regular pancakes because of the buttermilk. You can also add blueberries, apples or bits of crumbled bacon to the pancakes once the batter is on the griddle.

When my daughters were little, we would shape pancakes into animals, sailboats or whatever else they suggested. Try it with your own children, it's fun!

# Buttermilk Biscuits

❶ Sift all dry ingredients into large bowl.

❷ With pastry blender, cut in shortening until mixture resembles large crumbs.

❸ Add buttermilk (at room temperature) and stir until dough comes together.

❹ Turn out on floured board and knead for 1 minute. Roll $1/2$" thick. Cut out biscuit shapes; place on ungreased baking sheet. Brush tops of biscuits with a little extra buttermilk.

❺ Bake at 450°F for 12–15 minutes.

What a nice change from plain bread! I love the aroma that wafts through the kitchen while these are baking, it's so cozy.

### Ingredients
2C flour
2t baking powder
$1/2$t salt
$1/2$t baking soda
5T shortening
1C buttermilk

### Servings : 2 dozen biscuits

# French Toast

### Ingredients
2–4 eggs
1C milk
2T butter
4–8 slices of bread

❖

### Servings : 4 to 8 slices

❶ Beat eggs; add milk; blend together.
❷ Heat frying pan with 2T butter.
❸ Dip bread on both sides into egg mixture.
❹ Fry until golden brown; flip and cook other side.
❺ Serve with cinnamon sugar, fruit, maple syrup or jelly.

My girls all loved this; it's great for breakfast or for "supper snacks." Two eggs are sufficient for four slices of bread, use more eggs for additional slices. I loved eating this dish made with French bread and topped with strawberries when we travelled to San Francisco.

# Cinnamon Toast

### Ingredients
4T sugar
$^1/_2$t cinnamon
4T butter or margarine
4–6 slices American bread, toasted

❖

### Servings : 4 to 6 slices

❶ Blend butter, sugar and cinnamon.
❷ Spread on toasted bread.
❸ Broil just until sugar bubbles. Be careful not to burn! Serve immediately.

I'm sure my girls remember having this treat when they were little. You can use less sugar or more cinnamon if you prefer.

# Waffles

❶ Beat egg yolks in a bowl; beat in milk, melted butter and vanilla.

❷ Sift together all dry ingredients to combine. Add to liquid mixture; beat well.

❸ Beat egg whites until stiff peaks form; fold into batter.

❹ Bake 3 minutes in waffle iron.

This is one of Rudy's favorite special breakfasts. He loves waffles.

## Ingredients

4 eggs, separated

2C milk

4T melted butter

1t vanilla

2C flour

1t baking soda

2t baking powder

$\frac{1}{2}$t salt

1T sugar

## Servings : 12 waffles

# Toad in a Hole

## Ingredients

4 slices American bread

4T butter

4 eggs

---

## Servings : 2

❶ With tip of knife or round biscuit cutter, cut a circle in center of each bread slice. Melt butter in frying pan.

❷ Add bread. Brown; flip and brown other side.

❸ Add 1 egg in center hole. Cook until set; flip and cook other side to set.

# Foccaccia

❶ Stir yeast into warm water in mixer
   bowl. Let stand until creamy,
   approximately 10 minutes.

❷ Stir oil and $2^1/_4$C plus 1T water at
   room temperature into the yeast mix.

❸ Add 2C of the flour and salt; stir
   until smooth. Stir in remaining
   flour, 1C at a time, until dough comes
   together. Knead on floured board
   until velvety and soft.

❹ First Rise: Place dough in an oiled
   bowl; cover with plastic wrap. Let
   rise until doubled, approximately
   90 minutes.

❺ Second Rise: Cut dough into 3 pieces;
   shape into circles. Roll on floured
   board. Place on oiled 10" pie plate.
   Cover with towel; let rise 30 minutes.

❻ Third Rise: Dimple dough with your
   fingertips. Cover with moist towels and
   let rise until doubled, approximately
   2 hours. Add toppings: oil and salted
   water are the typical choices but you
   can also add sauce and cheese and
   make scrumptious foccaccia pizza.

❼ Bake 20–25 minutes at 400°F.

## Ingredients

1 pkg dry yeast
$^1/_4$C warm water
2T olive oil
$2^1/_4$C plus 1–2T
lukewarm water
$7^1/_2$C flour
1T salt

## Servings : 8

## PERFECT DAY

Grandmother on a winter's day
milked the cows and fed them hay,
slopped the hogs and saddled the mule,
and got the children off to school.

Did a washing, mopped the floors,
washed the windows, did some chores.
Cooked a dish of home dried fruit,
pressed her husband's Sunday suit.

Swept the parlor, made the bed,
baked a dozen loaves of bread.
Split some firewood and lugged it in
enough to fill the kitchen bin.

Cleaned the lamps and put in oil,
stewed some apples she thought might spoil.
Gathered the eggs and locked the stable,
back to the house and set the table.
Cooked a supper that was delicious,
and afterwards washed the dishes.

Fed the cat and sprinkled the clothes,
mended a basketful of hose.
Then sang to the children while they played
"When you come to the end of a perfect day."

Anonymous

This was a typical "Little Nonna" day,
but our days can be almost as busy.

# Basic Dough for Ravioli or Noodles

### Ingredients
3½C flour
4 eggs
1T salt
4-5T water
1t olive oil

Servings : 100 ravioli

❶ Place flour, salt, eggs and water in large bowl.
❷ Blend until a smooth, elastic dough forms.
❸ Wrap in plastic. Chill in refrigerator for 30 minutes.
❹ Roll pieces through pasta machine, beginning at the widest setting, and continue rolling through machine at progressively narrower notches to the last notch. Lightly sprinkle flour on board.
❺ Cut to form noodles or fill with spinach or meat for ravioli.

This is the dough I use for anolini and ravioli. To make green noodles, substitute spinach water for regular water.

# Ravioli Filling (Ripieno)

❶ Cook spinach in very little water in covered pan. Drain, squeezing out as much water as possible.

❷ Add cream cheese, salt, pepper and Parmesan cheese. Blend well.

❸ Sauté onion in butter; add to spinach.

❹ Add egg; blend everything thoroughly. Chill until ready to use.

❺ Roll out dough in strips. Place filling in small heaps along one side of strip; fold other side over filling. Press out air around each. Cut into little squares.

❻ To freeze ravioli, separate layers on a tray with aluminum foil, sprinkling corn meal over each foil layer. Wrap entire tray well, then place in freezer.

❼ To cook: Put ravioli into boiling, salted water for 12–15 minutes.

## Ingredients

3–4 pkgs. frozen chopped spinach

1 8 oz. pkg cream cheese

salt

pepper

1 1/2 C Parmesan cheese

3 T butter

1 onion, finely-chopped

1 egg

How many happy memories do ravioli and anolini bring to mind? They were served at almost every holiday, birthday or special celebration. Everyone enjoyed them with a good tomato sauce or just butter and cheese. This filling can also be used for Stuffed Onions (see p.64).

Ripieno is the filling placed in a buttered, crumb-covered pan. Bake at 400°F for 30 minutes; this will give you a spinach loaf. Use as a vegetable dish with roast chicken or in place of stuffing for chicken.

# Cannelloni

## Ingredients/Crêpe Batter

1 C cold water
1 C cold milk
4 eggs
½ t salt
1 C flour
¼ C butter, melted

---

## Servings : 6 to 7

❶ Place water, milk, eggs and salt in a bowl; beat well. Add flour and butter; blend. Cover and refrigerate overnight (or at least 3 hours). Consistency-wise, batter should resemble thin cream.

❷ Brush 6" skillet with olive oil. Heat pan until very hot (test by dropping water on skillet, if water forms drops and skips, the temperature is correct).

❸ Put 2 T batter in center of pan and quickly tilt pan in all directions to cover bottom. Return pan to heat for 70 seconds. Lift edge to see if it is light brown, then carefully turn and cook for 30 seconds on other side.

❹ Slide crepe onto wax paper and set aside. Re-oil pan and repeat process until all batter is used.

Note: Prior to filling, crepes can be frozen. Or, make a day ahead of time, then store in refrigerator, covered.

❶ Sauce: Brown onions in butter and olive oil. Add meat and bay leaves; cook slowly for 10 minutes. Add seasonings; cook for 5 minutes. Add tomatoes; simmer for 30 minutes. Stir; add tomato paste. Cook for 25 minutes.

❷ Filling: Spinach must be very well drained. Blend all ingredients together; season as desired.

❸ Spread filling evenly across center of each crepe. Roll or fold neatly.

❹ Place in a buttered baking pan; spoon meat sauce over crepes to cover. Sprinkle with grated cheese. Bake at 350°F for 12 minutes. Serve 2 cannelloni per person.

## Ingredients/Sauce and Filling:

2–3 onions, diced
$\frac{1}{4}$C butter
$\frac{1}{4}$C olive oil
1 lb cooked chopped chicken, meat, sausage or a blend
2 bay leaves
salt and pepper to taste
$1\frac{1}{2}$ lbs peeled plum tomatoes
1 T tomato paste
1 lb fresh spinach or 1 pkg cooked frozen spinach
2 eggs
$\frac{1}{2}$C grated cheese

# The Three Tortas

These are wonderful "veggie" meals that my mother (Little Nonna) and Rudy's mother (Big Nonna) would often make, and which I learned by trial and error. Big Nonna's Spinach Torta basically uses a pasta dough for the crust, and any left-over dough can be cut into noodles. Little Nonna's dough is more like a pie dough. The important thing to remember is to roll it thin, $1/8"$ or so. Always preheat your oven and use the best ingredients—it does make a difference. And don't lose your patience—practice makes perfect.

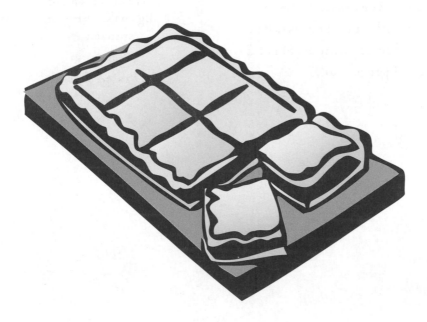

# Mom's Torta di Patate

❶ Blend all ingredients until dough holds together. Wrap in plastic wrap; chill 30 minutes.

❷ Oil the bottom of a rectangular baking or roasting pan. Roll out dough to ⅛" thick. (I roll this dough somewhat larger than the pan I use, then use the overlap to cover the filling.) Place in pan; trim if necessary and brush top with oil before placing in the oven.

### Ingredients/Dough
2¼ C flour
⅓ C olive oil
½ t salt
⅔ C warm water

### Servings: 16 pieces

❶ Make instant potatoes according to directions on package.

❷ Chop leek or onion; fry in butter until golden. Add to cooked instant potatoes.

❸ Add cream cheese and dash of pepper; blend until smooth.

❹ Add egg and Parmesan cheese. Blend well; spoon into dough-lined pan. Cover with overlapping dough and bake 30-45 minutes at 375°F or until dough is browned.

### Ingredients/Filling
1 envelope instant mashed potatoes
1 sm leek, white and green parts, or 1 onion
4 T butter
1 8-oz pkg cream cheese
pepper
1 egg
1 C Parmesan cheese

# Little Nonna's Torta di Riso

## Ingredients/Dough

2$\frac{1}{4}$C flour
$\frac{2}{3}$C warm water
(approximately)
$\frac{1}{2}$t salt
$\frac{1}{3}$C olive oil

Servings : 16 pieces

❶ Blend all ingredients until dough holds together.
❷ Wrap in plastic; chill 30 minutes.
❸ Roll out on floured board until larger than bottom of rectangular baking or roasting pan you will use. The overlap will cover torta filling.
❹ Oil bottom of pan. Lay dough in pan; fill.

## Ingredients/Filling

2C cooked rice
2C ricotta or 1C ricotta+ 1 egg
8-oz pkg cream cheese
1$\frac{1}{2}$C Parmesan cheese
black pepper
1 grated lemon rind + juice of that lemon (optional)

❶ Cook rice according to directions on package; don't forget to add salt to the water.
❷ Drain well. Add ricotta, egg, cheese and black pepper to taste; blend well.
❸ If desired, add lemon rind and juice; stir to incorporate.
❹ Spoon atop dough in pan; cover filling with remaining dough; brush with oil.
❺ Prick top crust with fork. Bake 30-45 minutes at 400°F until golden brown.

I like to add 1 large or 2 small zucchinis, cored and sliced, to the rice as it cooks. This keeps the rice moist and adds color.

# Big Nonna's Torta di Spinacci

❶ Blend all ingredients until dough holds together. Wrap in plastic; chill 30 minutes.

❷ Roll out thinly (I use the pasta machine). Oil bottom of a large, rectangular baking or roasting pan. Overlap dough strips in pan.

### Ingredients/Pasta

1 egg
2¼ C flour
¼ t salt
4 T olive oil
½ C water

---

### Servings : 16 pieces

❶ Wash spinach; remove stems.

❷ Place in just-cleaned, empty dish drainer and sprinkle with salt. Toss; let drain for 30 minutes.

❸ Squeeze as much water out of spinach as you can.

❹ Chop spinach; place in a large bowl or pot. Add oil; toss. Add cheese; toss.

❺ Pour into dough-lined pan. Cover top with dough strips; prick with a fork, brush with oil. Bake at 450°F for 15 minutes. Reduce heat to 400°F; bake an additional 25 minutes or until crust is golden brown.

I save the stems and cook them as a veggie. Any leftover dough can be cut into noodles.

### Ingredients/Filling

3 bags spinach
1 T salt*
¼ C olive oil
1½ C Parmesan cheese

---

*I use 1T
(Big Nonna uses 2T)

# Anolini

## Ingredients

2 lbs veal stew meat
$^1/_2$ lb beef stew meat
lemon juice
1t salt
pepper
$^1/_2$lb butter
1 lg onion, chopped
3 celery stalks, chopped
1 lg carrot
pinch rosemary
$^1/_2$ to 1C white wine
2–3 eggs
2C Parmesan cheese

---

## Servings:
## Approximately
## 500 anolini

Note: Dough recipe same as for Ravioli (see p.34).

❶ Sprinkle gristle-free meat with lemon juice; dry. Add salt and pepper.
❷ Sauté in butter until lightly browned.
❸ Brown onion, celery, carrot and rosemary.
❹ Add wine and simmer slowly, at least 2–3 hours, until tender.
❺ Grind everything together.
❻ Add eggs, grated cheese; correct seasonings.
❼ Chill approximately 3 hours or overnight. When ready to use, shape small balls approximately $^1/_2$" in size. Place on rolled-out dough as you do for ravioli (only much smaller) and cut.
❽ Anolini may be frozen or cooked in boiling broth for 10 minutes.

This is Big Nonna's specialty. She always makes them for holidays, and everyone looks forward to having them.

# Gnocchi

**❶** Make potatoes following package directions but omit butter.

**❷** Add egg; blend.

**❸** Add flour; blend until dough forms.

**❹** On a floured board, cut a piece of dough and roll into a long cylindrical strip.

**❺** Cut cylinder into 1" pieces and roll each piece off a floured fork.

**❻** Put gnocchi into a pot of boiling water. When they float to the top, they are done. Skim cooked gnocchi off with slotted spoon and place in large bowl with a good tomato sauce. Sprinkle with cheese.

To prevent dough from sticking, keep your hands, board and fork floured. Gnocchi are easy to make and quick to cook but can be tricky to roll out. No matter, they are delicious. Rudy's stepfather, Nonno Giletti, loves these; Big Nonna doesn't and never makes them. My mother used cooked, mashed fresh potatoes. I've found that instant potatoes yield more consistent results and are less time-consuming.

## Ingredients

1 envelope instant mashed potatoes

1 egg

1C flour

### Servings : 4 to 6

# Risotto

## Ingredients

1 16oz. can chicken broth
app. 1–3C tomato sauce
1 onion, chopped
2T olive oil
2–4T butter
2C arborio rice
parsley (optional)
$^{1}/_{2}$C red or 1C white wine
1C Parmesan cheese
pepper (to taste)

### Servings : 4 to 6

❶ Simmer broth in a saucepan.

❷ Simmer tomato sauce in a second saucepan.

❸ Sauté onion in oil and butter (soffritto) in a large pot.

❹ Add rice to the pot; blend into soffritto. You may add a little chopped parsley if desired. Add wine, stir.

❺ Add a little boiling broth to rice mixture; mix until absorbed.

❻ Add a little tomato sauce to rice mixture; mix until absorbed.

❼ Keep adding alternating boiling broth and tomato sauce until finished.

❽ If you need more liquid, you may add some boiling water.

❾ When cooked, add grated cheese, pepper and possibly more butter. Taste and correct.

The correct consistancy of this dish is hard to achieve even for an experienced cook . Don't get discouraged, you may have to try it a few times before you get it right. You want the final product to be more moist than dry. Cooking takes approximately 20–30 minutes. You can add peas or serve with stew, sausages, etc. This is a satisfying, delicious way to have rice. You can also add prosciutto or ham to the soffritto. Any of these extras add additional flavor.

# Fettuccine al Limone

❶ Lemon Sauce: Put butter and cream into a pot large enough to accommodate pasta later. Turn heat to High; when cream begins to boil, add lemon juice and peel; stir thoroughly. Continue to stir while cream reduces by half, then turn off heat. Toss pasta in this sauce.

❷ Pasta: While cream is reducing, drop pasta into a pot of boiling, salted water. When cooked, drain and transfer to pan with lemon sauce. Turn on heat to Medium; toss. Add grated cheese; toss again and serve with more cheese.

Little Nonna used lemon in her rice dishes at times and it's a nice change in this noodle dish. Try this different, quick sauce sometime—you'll like it!

## Ingredients
4T butter
1C heavy cream
2T fresh lemon juice
grated peel of 2 lemons
1 lb fettuccini
$\frac{1}{2}$C Parmesan cheese

### Servings : 4 to 6

# Pigai

## Ingredients

1 lb penne or farfalle pasta

2 C ricotta

$\frac{1}{2}$-1 C Parmesan cheese

$\frac{1}{4}$ C cream

$\frac{1}{2}$-1 C walnuts, finely chopped

salt and pepper

## Servings : 6

❶ Cook pasta in boiling, salted water for approximately 15 minutes.

❷ Mix ricotta, cheese, cream, nuts, salt and pepper in large bowl until well-blended. Toss cooked pasta with cheese mix. Serve with additional Parmesan cheese.

This recipe was served by mother's friend Jenny on New Year's Day.

# Rudy's Polenta with 3 Cheeses

❶ Bring water to a full boil. Add salt,
   oil and butter.

❷ Slowly whisk in cornmeal (to prevent
   lumping) until completely blended.

❸ Stir constantly with wooden spoon,
   briefly halting stirring every 15
   minutes or so. Continue this cycle for
   approximately 60 minutes; at this
   point, polenta should separate from
   the sides of the pot and be fully cooked.

❹ Add all cheeses after polenta has
   cooked for 30 minutes; continue to
   stir until cheeses melt. Pour polenta
   out into a large bowl when cooked.

❺ Soak pot overnight in warm water
   to clean.

I remember hating polenta when I was a young
girl. I would ask for a piece of bread when my
mother made it. Then Big Nonna discovered another version of the "old standby" on a trip to
Piemonte, Italy. It included four cheeses and I've
liked it ever since. This is something Rudy makes
on cold winter days and I'll make a nice stew (see
p.85) to serve with it. It's Northern Italian soul
food! A nice glass of Barbera or Barolo (red wine)
is good with this combination. It's cornmeal mush
at its best!!

For a tasty lunch or snack, leftover polenta
can be sliced and fried in a pan with a little olive
oil and slices of Muenster cheese on top.

## Ingredients

4 qts. water

1 T salt

1 T oil

1 T butter

1 1/2 lb box cornmeal

1 C Muenster cheese

1 C Jarlsberg cheese

1 C Parmesan cheese

## Servings : 8 to 10

# Bomba (Italian Rice Mold)

### Ingredients/
### sugo-stew :

1 lg onion, chopped

2 lbs veal cubes or boned
chicken

$1/2$ C mushrooms

$1/4$ lb butter

pinch of
rosemary/thyme/sage

1t salt

pepper

1t tomato paste

$1/2$ C white wine

1 can of tomatoes, crushed

1–2C broth or water

## Servings : 8 to 10

❶ Sauté onion, meat and mushrooms until browned. Add herbs, salt and pepper.

❷ Add tomato paste; blend. Add wine, then bring to a quick boil for 1 minute.

❸ Reduce heat to Medium. Add tomatoes.

❹ Add broth or water. Cook uncovered for 30 minutes, then cover and cook until done, 1–2 hours.

❶ Cook rice for 8 minutes.
❷ Drain and add eggs, grated cheese, salt, pepper and some stew sauce.
❸ Grease deep pan with butter; sprinkle with bread crumbs.
❹ Pour rice in pan and around sides.
❺ Fill center with stew; cover with rice.
❻ Bake 30 minutes at 375°F until golden on top.
❼ Loosen sides with a spatula. Turn out within 5 minutes.

This is a little time-consuming but it's always a hit. It looks like a beautiful cake. Serve extra stew on the side. I brought it to a picnic once, and all my friends asked for the recipe.

## Ingredients/rice:

1 lb rice

3 eggs

1C grated cheese

salt and pepper

stew sauce without meat

---

# Crustless Quiche

## Ingredients
1C chopped onion
chopped parsley
$\frac{1}{2}$C oil
3–4 eggs
salt and pepper
1C biscuit mix
$\frac{1}{2}$C Parmesan cheese
3C chopped zucchini

## Servings : 4 to 6

*If you don't have an instant
biscuit mix, you can use
the following:
1C flour, 1t baking powder, a
pinch of salt and pepper

❶ Fry the onion and parsley in $\frac{1}{4}$C of the oil.

❷ Beat eggs with remaining $\frac{1}{4}$C oil, plus salt and pepper.

❸ Add onion to egg mix; blend.

❹ Add biscuit mix and cheese, blend.

❺ Add zucchini; blend. Pour into well-greased pie pan.

❻ Bake at 350°F for 30 minutes.

This is a quick vegetable-based meal. I make it often in the summer when Rudy's garden is so full of zucchini that I can't keep up with using them.

When you prepare the zucchini, don't peel but do core—meaning, remove the seeds—before dicing. This keeps them firm, not mushy, and saves you from chewing on seeds.

# Pizza Rustica

① Combine flour, sugar and baking
   powder; cut in butter until flour
   is mealy.
② Add eggs; blend into a soft dough.
   Let rest under a bowl for 10 minutes.
③ When rolling out, be sure to flour
   both sides of dough; it should be
   ½" thick.  Grease bottom of a 9"x9"
   pan; place dough in pan.

## Ingredients/Pasta Frolla Dough

2C flour
2T sugar
2t baking powder
¼ lb butter
2 eggs
1 additional egg yolk

### Servings : 8 to 10

① Beat ricotta with eggs until smooth.
② Add all other ingredients; mix well.
③ Pour into 9"x9" pan lined with pasta
   frolla.
④ Cover with remaining dough. Brush
   top with egg yolk.
⑤ Prick top of crust with fork. Bake
   15 minutes at 400°F. Reduce heat
   to 325°F; bake for an additional
   45–55 minutes. Let cool in oven.
   To serve, cut into squares.

Serve either warm or cold for an appealing
appetizer. This dish can be frozen and reheated
later if desired.

## Ingredients/Pizza Filling :

2 lb ricotta
4 eggs
½ lb sweet sausage,
chopped and fried
½C Parmesan cheese
½ lb cubed mozzarella
pepper
¼ lb prosciutto or ham,
chopped
parsley and herbs

# Manicotti (Little Muffs)

## Ingredients/Crêpes

1¹/₂ C milk
3 eggs
1C flour
1T melted butter
¹/₂t salt

### Servings : 4 to 6

❶ Blend all ingredients until smooth. Let stand 30 minutes.

❷ Heat small frying pan with sloped sides; brush with butter. Pour in 2T batter; tip and swirl pan to cover bottom with a thin layer. When browned, turn with spatula to brown other side. Remove and set aside; repeat process until all batter is used.

I turn them out onto waxed paper, then stack and freeze for later use. As a dessert you can serve them sprinkled with confectioners' sugar or with fruit or ice cream; use your imagination.

❶ Make soffritto by sautéing onion, parsley and herbs for 5 minutes.

❷ Add diced mushrooms and chicken breasts. Sauté until chicken is lightly browned and mushrooms are cooked.

❸ Add white wine to mixture; cook until wine evaporates. Add well-drained spinach; toss all together. Add cheese, salt and pepper.

❹ Fill each crêpe with 1 to 2T of mixture and roll as you would a typical jelly roll. Place in buttered pan, side by side.

❺ Pour cheese sauce or tomato sauce over crêpes and bake at 350°F for 30 minutes or until hot and bubbly.

## Ingredients/Filling

1 onion, chopped

parsley

herbs (rosemary, thyme, sage)

1 C chopped mushrooms

2–3 chicken breasts

$\frac{1}{2}$ C white wine

1 pkg chopped frozen spinach, cooked

$\frac{1}{2}$ C Parmesan cheese

cheese sauce (see p.77)

salt and pepper

The six most important words in the English language:
"I admit I made a mistake."
The five most important words in the English language:
"You did a good job."
The four most important words in the English language:
"What is your opinion?"
The three most important words in the English language:
"If you please."
The two most important words in the English language:
"Thank you."
The one most important word in the English language:
"We."
The least important words in the English language:
"I."

Anonymous

# Vegetables

# Zucchini Flowers

## Ingredients

2 eggs, well-beaten

pinch of salt

pepper

1t olive oil

³/₄C milk

³/₄C flour

1t baking powder

6T olive oil

24 male zucchini/
pumpkin flowers

## Servings : 4 to 6

❶ Beat eggs, salt, pepper, oil and milk together.

❷ When smooth, add flour and baking powder; blend thoroughly.

❸ Place 6T olive oil in large frying pan; heat but don't burn.

❹ Wash flowers; pat dry; carefully remove stamen. Dip flowers into batter; place in hot oil, being careful not to crowd pan.

❺ Cook over Medium heat until browned, approximately 3 minutes. Flip; brown other sides. Repeat process with remaining flowers.

❻ Serve hot.

Male flowers are the ones with longer stems; female flowers bear the zucchini. This is a real delicacy not familiar to many. We enjoyed these in the summer along with zucchini from Rudy's garden—and they have very few calories. Just be sure to use the male flower or you won't have zucchini in your garden.

# Sautéed Zucchini

❶ Wash and trim zucchini. Slice lengthwise; scoop out seeds; chop.

❷ Heat oil in frying pan; add onions to brown.

❸ Chop tomato; add it and garlic to onions. (This is optional.)

❹ Add zucchini, salt, pepper and parsley, blend. Cook until crisp-tender.

❺ Add vinegar; stir. Cook 2 minutes; take off heat. Serve.

### Ingredients

3 med zucchini
$^1/_2$C olive oil
1 onion, chopped
1 fresh tomato
1 clove garlic, mashed
salt and pepper
parsley
2T–$^1/_4$C wine vinegar

## Servings : 3 to 4

Be sure to scoop out seeds or zucchini will be mushy. This should take about 10 minutes to cook. Remember that you can also bake zucchini. Scoop out seeds, then fill with your favorite meat or veggie filling. Place in an oiled pan, dribble a little oil over filling. Bake at 325°F for 25 minutes. Zucchini are wonderful vegetables, you can do so many things with them.

# Stuffed Artichokes

## Ingredients

6 fresh artichokes
$^1/_2$ C chopped parsley
$^1/_2$ C Parmesan cheese
$^1/_2$ t salt
$^1/_2$ t pepper
$^1/_4$ C bread crumbs
7 T olive oil
$^1/_4$ t onion salt
pinch thyme
lemon juice
pinch garlic salt

## Servings : 6

❶ Wash artichokes; remove hard outer leaves. Cut off leaf tips and remove hairy interior; trim bottoms so artichokes sit flat in pan.

❷ Mix together parsley, cheese, salt, pepper, bread crumbs, 6 T olive oil, onion salt and thyme.

❸ Spreading leaves apart with fingertips, stuff in filling at random. Place artichokes side by side in large saucepan atop stove.

❹ Sprinkle with a little oil and lemon juice to prevent artichokes from discoloring.

❺ Cook with about 1" water and 1 T olive oil in pan bottom for 40 minutes on Medium heat or until a leaf pulls off easily.

A touch of garlic salt adds pizzazz. My daughter, Gigi, loves these, and so do I. Not everyone does. My husband feels it is too much work to eat.

# Artichoke Casserole

❶ Cook frozen artichokes or drain and
mash canned artichokes.
❷ Blend artichokes, mayonnaise and
Parmesan cheese.
❸ Spread in small baking pan.
❹ Bake for 20 minutes at 350°F.

If you like artichokes, you'll love this. Best of all,
it's so easy to make.

### Ingredients
2 pkgs frozen artichokes
(or 1 lg can artichokes)
1C mayonnaise
1C Parmesan cheese

---

### Servings : 6

# Artichoke Fritters

❶ Cook artichokes according to package
instructions, until tender. Drain well.
❷ Beat egg yolks; add milk; stir until
smooth.
❸ Place flour, salt, pepper and baking
powder in separate bowl; mix.
❹ Add beaten egg yolks and milk mixture
to dry ingredients; mix until smooth.
❺ Coat each artichoke in batter.
❻ Put ¼"–½" oil in bottom of frying
pan; heat until it is hot enough for
frying. Drop artichokes into pan,
being careful not to crowd. Fry until
golden; remove and set on paper towels to drain. Repeat with remaining
artichokes. Serve.

### Ingredients
2 pkgs frozen artichokes
3 egg yolks
1¼C milk
1½C flour
salt and pepper
¾t baking powder
oil

---

### Servings : 6 to 8

# Asparagus

### Ingredients
2 lbs fresh asparagus
butter
Parmesan cheese

### Servings : 4 to 5

❶ Wash stalks; cut off ends up to purple or green part. Scrape off scales.

❷ Put into enough boiling, salted water to cover (unless you prefer to steam).

❸ Cook for 12 minutes; drain well. Put on heatproof plate you've warmed in the oven. Spoon on melted butter; sprinkle with Parmesan cheese. Serve.

My father, Nonno of Staten Island, loved asparagus topped with two poached or fried eggs; that's a meal in itself. This springtime veggie is also good cold with vinaigrette dressing.

# Sautéed Cabbage

### Ingredients
4T olive oil
1 onion, chopped
$^1/_2$ sm Savoy cabbage, shredded
$^1/_2$ t salt
pepper
dill and parsley to taste (optional)
1 sm apple, peeled and diced
2T vinegar

### Servings : 4

❶ Heat oil; add chopped onion; cook until brown.

❷ Add shredded cabbage, salt, pepper, dill, parsley and apple. Stir.

❸ Brown, then sprinkle with vinegar. Mix; cover; cook 15-20 minutes.

I like to serve this Vitamin C-packed dish with pork dishes. You can use any cabbage, even red; just aim to avoid using the hard parts of the leaves.

# Stuffed Cabbage

❶ Blanch cabbage leaves by pouring
boiling water over them.

❷ Cut out hard ribs of cabbage leaves.
Let sit.

❸ Cook rice according to package
directions; drain well.

❹ Sauté onion, parsley and herbs in oil.
Remove to a bowl; set aside.

❺ Sauté chopped meat in same pan. Add
onion mixture, garlic salt, salt and
pepper; stir.

❻ Blend rice into meat mixture. Add
$1/4$C tomato sauce; blend. Add egg;
blend.

❼ Place large spoonful of filling on each
leaf; fold to cover.

❽ Heat 2T oil in large pan. Place rolls
side by side; brown on both sides.
Add remaining tomato sauce to pan.

❾ Cover pan; cook for 15 minutes over
Medium heat. Check to prevent
scorching; if liquid gets too low, add
water or more sauce.

This satisfying winter dish is a complete meal. I
know that some of my family members hated the
cabbage but liked the filling.

## Ingredients

12 Savoy cabbage leaves
$1/2$C rice
1 sm onion, chopped
parsley, thyme and sage
to taste
$1/4$ lb chopped meat
$1/2$t salt
pinch pepper
dash garlic salt
$1/2$C tomato sauce
1 egg
2T olive oil

### Servings : 6

# Sweet and Sour Cabbage

## Ingredients

9 slices bacon

1 med to lg onion, sliced

4 bay leaves

12 peppercorns

9T vinegar

2T sugar

1C water

2 lbs cabbage

1T salt

1t caraway seeds (optional)

## Servings : 4

❶ In a heavy pot, render bacon. Add sliced onion; simmer slowly.

❷ Add bay leaves, peppercorns, vinegar, sugar and water; simmer slowly. It should now have a sweet-and-sour taste.

❸ Shred cabbage; add to above.

❹ Add salt and caraway seeds. Simmer slowly for 1 hour or until tender, stirring occasionally.

# Stuffed Peppers

❶ Wash peppers; cut stem off each; remove seeds. Drop into boiling water for 1 minute, drain.

❷ Cook rice according to package directions; drain.

❸ Place oil in pan; heat. Add onion; brown.

❹ Add meat to onion, stirring to break up any lumps. (If using sausages, remove casings.) Add salt, pepper, garlic salt; brown.

❺ Mix meat with cooked rice, egg, cheese and $^1/_4$C tomato sauce. Blend well.

❻ Spoon filling into peppers; place side by side in oiled baking pan. Top with remaining tomato sauce.

❼ Bake approximately 45 minutes at 400°F.

❽ Check pan periodically; add a little water or broth if very dry.

## Ingredients

4 green bell peppers
1 $^1/_2$C rice
2T olive oil
1C finely-chopped onion
$^1/_4$ lb chopped meat or
8 sausages
salt and pepper
pinch garlic salt
1 egg
$^1/_4$C Parmesan cheese
$^1/_2$C tomato sauce

## Servings: 4

# Stuffed Onions

## Ingredients

2 lg onions, peeled
2 pkgs frozen chopped
spinach
1 8-oz pkg cream cheese
$^1/_2$t salt
pepper
1C Parmesan cheese
1 egg
4T butter
2T oil

## Servings: 2 to 3

❶ Cut onions in half. Remove center sections to create hollow "shells;" place in boiling water. Cover; cook for 10 minutes. Drain; let cool. If desired, save centers for another use.

❷ Cook spinach according to package directions, then drain thoroughly. Cool; squeeze out any excess water.

❸ Add cream cheese, salt, pepper, Parmesan cheese and egg to spinach. Blend well.

❹ Fill each onion shell with spinach filling. Gently bend onion edges over to cover filling.

❺ Heat butter and oil. Add onions; brown on each side for approximately 15 minutes.

This is another delicious vegetarian meal. Offer slices of crusty bread to pick up the pan juices. You can serve as a light luncheon or as a vegetable with something else. Depending on the size of the onions, you may need more than two.

# Eggplant alla zia Mary

❶ Wash and dry eggplant; do not peel. Cut into thin $1/4"$-round slices.

❷ Place slices on brown paper or on paper towel; sprinkle lightly with salt. Let drain for 30 minutes.

❸ Pat dry; sprinkle lightly with flour; shake off excess.

❹ Heat oil in pan, preferably a non-stick one. Add eggplant slices; brown on both sides.

❺ Stack eggplant slices pancake-style with thin slices of cheese in between each; sprinkle with pepper. Serve hot. You may place eggplant stacks in a warm oven while you cook the rest of the batch.

This was my aunt's favorite way to serve eggplant. However, in many ways, it's similar to Eggplant Parmigiana (see p. 66) without salsa.

## Ingredients

1 med eggplant
salt
flour for dipping
4T oil
1 pkg Muenster or mozzarella
pepper

## Servings : 3 to 4

# Eggplant Parmigiana

## Ingredients

2 med eggplants
1t salt
$^{1}/_{2}$C flour
2 eggs, well beaten
$^{1}/_{2}$C bread crumbs
herbs (basil, parsley)
6T olive oil
$^{1}/_{4}$C melted butter
1t pepper
3C tomato sauce
$^{1}/_{2}$C Parmesan cheese
sliced Muenster or
mozzarella

## Servings : 6

❶ Wash eggplant; do not peel. Cut into $^{1}/_{2}$" slices.

❷ Sprinkle with salt. Place on paper towel; let drain for 30 minutes; pat dry.

❸ Sprinkle slices with flour; dip in beaten eggs.

❹ Dip into bread crumbs and herbs.

❺ Combine oil and butter in pan; heat.

❻ Add eggplant; sprinkle with salt and pepper. Sauté until medium brown, approximately 5 minutes each side.

❼ Preheat oven to 350°F. Oil a baking pan; cover bottom of pan with a thin layer of sauce.

❽ Arrange slices atop sauce. Sprinkle with Parmesan cheese; place 1 thin slice mozzarella on each piece of eggplant. Spoon more sauce over cheese, then continue layering process using ingredients. Bake 30 minutes or until bubbly.

This is a great dish to prepare when company's coming! You can make and freeze it before it's cooked, or make it a day ahead, refrigerate and then bake when needed. It's like veggie lasagna.

# Finocchio (Fennel)

❶ Trim bottoms and tough outer leaves of fennel. Wash; cut into quarters.

❷ Drop into boiling, salted water and cook until tender, approximately 15 minutes.

❸ Drain well. Place in buttered pan; sprinkle with pepper and Parmesan cheese.

### Ingredients

2 good-sized finocchio (fennel)

butter

pepper

Parmesan cheese

### Servings : 4

This is a winter veggie. We traditionally have it on Thanksgiving, Christmas and New Year's. They can be cooked a day ahead and then put in the oven with butter and cheese the next day. You can also serve them raw, as you would celery sticks, with a nice vinaigrette dressing. We had it that way when I was a little girl. It's crunchy and has a slight licorice flavor. Try it both ways.

# Mushrooms Trifolati

## Ingredients

1 lb mushrooms
$\frac{1}{4}$ C butter
1 onion, chopped
chopped parsley
salt and pepper
$\frac{1}{4}$ C white wine

## Servings : 4

❶ Wash mushrooms; let dry. Slice thinly.

❷ Heat butter in skillet; add onion and parsley; cook until soft.

❸ Add mushrooms; stir; sprinkle with salt and pepper. Cook slowly for 20 minutes.

❹ Turn up heat. When mushroom mixture sizzles, add wine. Cook for 3 minutes.

This is a great side dish for an omelet or meat. I've always loved mushrooms, I eat them like this with a nice slice of Italian bread for scooping up the juices.

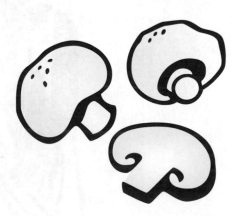

# Baked Mushrooms

❶ Wash mushrooms; let dry. Remove
   stems from caps; set caps aside. Chop
   stems finely; sauté in butter.
❷ Mix cheese, bread crumbs, chopped
   parsley, prosciutto, sautéed mushroom
   stems, salt, pepper and onion salt.
   Taste for correct seasoning.
❸ Spoon mixture into reserved caps,
   place on an oiled pan.  Bake 45 minutes
   or less at 325°F.

## Ingredients

12 lg mushrooms
2T butter
2T Parmesan cheese
2T bread crumbs
parsley (leaves only)
4 slices prosciutto*,
   chopped finely
pinch of salt
pepper
pinch of onion or
   garlic salt
3T oil

Servings: 6

*Bacon or ham
may be substituted
for the prosciutto.

# Potato Salad I

### Ingredients

7 potatoes, boiled
$^1/_4$t onion salt
1 green pepper, chopped
chopped parsley
3 celery stalks, chopped
1 carrot, shredded
4 hard-cooked eggs
pepper
2T olive oil
4T vinegar
4–8 T mayonnaise*

## Servings : 6 to 8

\* I like to use "Dijonnaise,"
which is a mustard-mayo
combo, for zing.

❶ Slice potatoes into large pieces; place in large bowl.

❷ Sprinkle with onion salt, green pepper, parsley, celery and carrot; toss.

❸ Add sliced eggs, black pepper, oil, vinegar and mayonnaise.

❹ Toss together; correct seasonings. Refrigerate until serving.

Serve on a bed of lettuce, in lettuce cups or pass in a bowl.

# Potato Salad II

❶ Wash potatoes. Boil in large covered pot until you can pierce with knife, approximately 15 minutes. Take off heat. Run potatoes under cold water to stop cooking. Cut into chunks.

❷ In a large bowl, toss potatoes, oil and vinegar. Add celery, parsley, green pepper, salt, pepper, onion salt and pickle relish. Toss.

❸ Add mayonnaise and Dijonnaise; toss. Add eggs. Refrigerate to let flavors meld. Serve.

### Ingredients
15 med potatoes
oil and vinegar
2 celery stalks, chopped
chopped parsley
1 green pepper, chopped
· salt and pepper
onion salt to taste
1 T pickle relish
$\frac{1}{2}$ C mayonnaise
1t Dijonnaise (see p. 70)
3 hard-cooked eggs, chopped

### Servings : 8

# Home Fries

❶ Wash, peel and cube potatoes.

❷ Heat oil in saucepan; sauté onion and green pepper for 5 minutes.

❸ Add potatoes, salt, pepper and herbs to pan; sauté everything until potatoes are cooked through, approximately 20 minutes.

### Ingredients
3 lg potatoes
4 T olive oil
1 onion, chopped
1 green pepper, chopped
salt and pepper
parsley, sage, rosemary

### Servings : 3 to 4

# Potatoes Roesti

## Ingredients

3–4 baking potatoes
pepper
onion salt
rosemary or sage
4T olive oil

---

### Servings : 3 to 4

❶ Wash unpeeled potatoes; place in covered pot of boiling water for 5 minutes.

❷ Remove potatoes; place in cold water to stop cooking. When cool enough to handle, peel. Place in refrigerator overnight.

❸ Shred potatoes on a box grater. Sprinkle with onion salt, rosemary or sage and pepper.

❹ Heat oil in saucepan, preferably nonstick to make flipping easier.

❺ Add potatoes; press down all around with a wide spatula to create an even layer that covers the bottom of pan.

❻ Fry over Medium-High heat until potatoes are browned on bottom. Loosen around sides and bottom, then flip potato patty out onto a heated dish.

❼ Add more oil to hot frying pan, heat. Slide uncooked side of patty into hot oil; cook until browned.

❽ Loosen around edges; flip out onto heated platter. Cut into 4 servings.

This is a smart, satisfying way to use up cold leftover potatoes.

# Crisp Potato Pancakes

❶ Peel potatoes; shred finely on box grater. Place in bowl; cover with cold water; let stand for 5 minutes. Drain well in colander, then place potatoes on paper towel to continue draining.

❷ Add all remaining ingredients except for fat; stir gently to combine. Place fat in skillet; heat. Drop in mixture by tablespoonfuls; flatten with spatula to create thin cakes. Brown, then flip patties to brown other sides.

### Ingredients
4–5 med raw potatoes
1 med onion, grated
1 egg
$^3/_4$t salt
$^1/_4$t pepper
fat for frying

### Servings : 3 to 4

# Three Bean Salad

❶ Cook beans in boiling salted water until just tender; drain; let cool.

❷ Place beans in large bowl. Add carrot, relish and mayonnaise; stir. Season with salt and pepper. Garnish with onion rings or parsley.

### Ingredients
1 can kidney beans, washed and drained
1 10-oz pkg frozen cut green beans
1 10-oz pkg frozen wax beans (yellow)
1C shredded raw carrot
1T pickle relish
$^1/_2$C mayonnaise
salt and pepper
thinly-sliced red onion rings (optional)
parsley (optional)

### Servings : 6

# Leek Pie (Quiche)

## Ingredients/Dough

2 C flour
$^1/_2$ t salt
$^3/_4$ C butter
$^1/_4$ C cold water

### Servings : 6

❶ Combine all ingredients to form a dough. Wrap in plastic; chill 2 hours.
❷ Lightly flour work surface; roll out dough until large enough to cover 10" pie plate. Gently lay dough in plate.
❸ Take a piece of aluminum foil and shape it to fit over the dough like a cupcake liner. Note: Do not press foil into pie crust or it will stick.
❹ Place pie pan in oven; bake at 375°F for 15 minutes. Remove foil from crust; let cool.

## Ingredients/Filling

5 leeks, white part only
$^1/_4$ C butter
5 eggs
2 C half & half
$^1/_2$ t salt
$^1/_4$ t pepper

❶ Cut leeks into thin slices; sauté in butter for approximately 10 minutes. Spread over bottom of dough.
❷ Stir together eggs, half & half, salt and pepper. Pour over leeks. Bake at 375°F for 40–45 minutes or until firm and browned.

# Broccoli Fluff

❶ Cook broccoli according to instructions on package. Drain well.

❷ Beat yolks, salt and pepper together until creamy. Add flour; stir. Add mayonnaise, butter and cheese; mix. Stir in cooked broccoli.

❸ Beat egg whites until soft peaks form. Fold into broccoli mixture. Pour into a buttered Pyrex pie plate. Bake at 350°F for 30–40 minutes.

This is a nice side dish.

## Ingredients

2 10-oz pkgs chopped broccoli

3 eggs, separated

salt and pepper

1 T flour

1 C light mayonnaise

1 T butter

$\frac{1}{2}$ C Parmesan cheese

### Servings : 8

# Cranapple Sauce

### Ingredients
3–4 apples
1C water
1C sugar
1 pkg cranberries

---

### Servings : 8

❶ Wash, peel and core apples. Cut into quarters.
❷ Boil water and sugar until sugar dissolves.
❸ Add cranberries and apples.
❹ Cook until apples are soft and cranberries pop; stir gently to combine.
❺ Chill. Serve with poultry, pork or as fruit.


# Cranberry/Orange Relish

### Ingredients
4C cranberries
2 seeded, unpeeled oranges
2C sugar

---

### Servings : 2 pints

❶ Combine cranberries and oranges in work bowl of food processor. Remove to large bowl.
❷ Add sugar; stir to combine. Refrigerate overnight to allow flavors to blend.

# Cheese Sauce

❶ Melt butter in saucepan; add salt and
pepper. Remove from heat; stir in
flour until smooth. Slowly add milk,
stir. Place pan on Medium heat; stir
until mixture thickens. Add cheese;
continue cooking and stirring until
cheese melts and comes to a boil.

❷ Pour over macaroni; bake at 350°F
for 30 minutes.

## Ingredients

2 T butter*

$^1/_2$ t salt

$^1/_8$ t pepper

2 T flour*

2 C milk

1 $^1/_2$ C American or
Cheddar cheese

macaroni (optional)

## Servings : 6

* If you'd like, use sauce over
vegetables, such as broccoli
or cauliflower, or over toast.
Change flour and butter
quantities to 4T each
to yield a thicker sauce.

# Pesto alla Genovese

## Ingredients

5 cloves garlic, minced

$^1/_2$ C chopped basil
or parsley*

$^1/_2$ t salt

$^1/_4$ C Parmesan cheese

6–8T olive oil or minced
pancetta

2T pignoli nuts (optional)

## Servings : 6

\* Or $^1/_4$ C chopped basil and
$^1/_4$ C chopped parsley

❶ In a small bowl, mix together garlic, basil, cheese and salt.

❷ Beat mixture until smooth.

❸ Gradually add oil in a steady stream, working into a smooth paste.

This can be added to sauces, soups or meat dishes for extra flavor. It can also be tossed with noodles and butter. My aunt would add pignoli nuts; Little Nonna never did and neither do I. Pesto can also be frozen and used when needed or stored in the refrigerator with a thin layer of oil over the top.

# Tomato Sauce I (Bolognese)

❶ Soak mushrooms in tepid water for 15 minutes. Remove mushrooms, reserving water for later; squeeze; chop.

❷ Heat butter and oil in saucepan; sauté onions and prosciutto over Low heat until onions are golden.

❸ Add mushrooms and meat; cook until meat is browned.

❹ Add wine; cook for 5 minutes. Add mushroom water.

❺ Add tomatoes, tomato paste and broth.

❻ Allow sauce to simmer slowly until thickened, approximately 2 hours. Color should be dark as opposed to bright red.

This meaty sauce is great with spaghetti or macaroni.

## Ingredients

7 slices dried mushrooms*
2T butter
2T olive oil
2 lg onions, chopped
$1/4$ lb prosciutto, chopped
1 lb lean stew beef
$1/4$C red wine
1 large can plum tomatoes
2T tomato paste
1C broth or bouillon

## Servings : $1^{1}/_{4}$C

* Porcini mushrooms are optional. They're hard to find and expensive, but fabulous. My uncle used to send my mother a little package of these from Italy. He would go into the woods around Borgo Taro, a region famous for mushrooms, to find them. What a treasure they are! I'll never forget the mushroom dinner we had at a restaurant called Giovanni's in Borgo Taro many years ago.

# Tomato Sauce II

## Ingredients

1$^1/_2$ lbs tomatoes*
$^1/_4$ C butter
$^1/_4$ C olive oil
1 lg onion, diced
5–10 sprigs fresh parsley
2–3 sprigs fresh basil,
    chopped
1 small green pepper,
    chopped
veal or prosciutto
$^1/_2$ lb lean ground pork
$^3/_4$ C mushrooms
$^1/_4$ C wine or sherry
1t salt
$^1/_2$t pepper
garlic (optional)
1C broth

## Servings : 1$^1/_4$C

*approximately 4 cups canned
or 23 fresh Roma tomatoes

❶ Peel and chop tomatoes. In saucepan, make a soffritto with butter, oil, onions, parsley, basil and pepper over Medium heat; cook until golden brown.

❷ Add meat; brown. Add mushrooms; brown. Add wine; cook for 5 minutes.

❸ Add tomatoes, salt, pepper, garlic and chicken or beef broth. Simmer for 30–45 minutes over Low to Medium heat. Stir well; add tomato paste and stir again. Cook approximately 1 hour.

❹ Serve. Or, let cool, then freeze for another day.

When I use fresh tomatoes, I add 1 stalk chopped celery and 1 grated carrot to the soffritto. I also use 1T chicken bouillon instead of broth.

# Salsa Giardiniere con Pomidori Freshi (Garden-Style with Fresh Tomatoes)

❶ Make a soffrito with asterisked (*) items in frying pan over Medium heat; cook until onion is lightly browned.

❷ Add tomatoes; cook 5 minutes.

❸ Add wine/sherry over High heat; cook 5 additional minutes.

❹ Add bouillon, salt and pepper; cook over High heat to reduce, approximately 15 minutes.

## Ingredients

1 onion, chopped*
6 sprigs parsley*
6 basil leaves, minced*
1 green pepper, chopped*
1 sm carrot, chopped*
1 celery stalk, chopped*
4T olive oil*
4T butter*
6 fresh tomatoes, blanched and quartered
4T dry sherry or red wine
1 bouillon cube (chicken or beef)

### Servings : 1C

## SERENITY PRAYER

God, grant me the serenity
to accept the things I cannot change;
give me courage
to change things which must be changed;
and the wisdom
to distinguish one from the other.

Reinhold Mebuhr

---

*"Non ti scordar di me*          (Don't forget me)
*la vita mia legatà a te*   (My life is bound to you)
*Ti amo sempre più*          (I love you ever more)
*C'è sempre un nido*          (There's always a place
*nel mio cuor per te*          in my heart for you)
*Non ti scordar di me"*          (Don't forget me)

a verse from Non ti Scordar di Me

It's an old Italian love song very dear to me and Rudy.

# Meats & Fish

# Meatballs

## Ingredients

1¹/₂ lbs chopped mixed
meat (beef, veal, pork)

onion salt

¹/₂ t salt

pepper

parsley, thyme and sage

¹/₂ C Parmesan cheese

¹/₂ C milk

¹/₄ C bread crumbs or 2
slices white bread

1 egg

Servings : 6 to 8

❶ Place meat in large bowl; add onion
salt, salt, pepper, chopped parsley,
thyme, sage and cheese. Mix.

❷ Place milk in different bowl; add
bread; let milk absorb. Add egg and
bread; mix thoroughly. Shape into
small balls.

❸ Add meatballs to simmering tomato
sauce (see p. 79, 80).

❹ Simmer 45 minutes.

I don't brown my meatballs prior to adding them
to sauce, so they are less greasy. However, if you
like, brown in 2T oil.

# Meatloaf

## Ingredients

Same as for Meatballs
(recipe above)

tomato sauce

cheese (optional)

Servings : 6 to 8

❶ Pack meatball mixture into a loaf pan.

❷ Cover loaf with tomato sauce. Or, if
desired, put a slice of cheese on top
during last 10 minutes of baking.

❸ Bake at 350°F for 45 minutes to
1 hour.

One variation I like: Put half the meat mixture
into a loaf pan. On top, lay 3 shelled, hard-cooked
eggs, then cover with the rest of the meat.

# Veal Stew

❶ Cut veal into 2" cubes. Combine flour, salt and pepper in plastic bag. Place a few meat pieces in bag; shake to lightly coat. Remove; set aside. Repeat with remaining meat until all pieces are coated.

❷ In a large pot, heat 2T butter and 1T oil. Brown meat a few pieces at a time, adding more oil if needed. Transfer pieces to a plate as they brown.

❸ Reduce heat. Sauté onion until golden. Return veal to pan; add garlic and herbs.

❹ Add wine; cook for 4 minutes; add broth and sauce. Bring mixture to a boil. Reduce heat; simmer, partially covered, until meat is tender, approximately 2 hours.

❺ Melt 2T butter in skillet. Sauté parsley and mushrooms until golden; stir into stew. Serve.

I sometimes add peeled, cubed potatoes, frozen pearl or small onions and a few small carrots for the last hour of cooking. Beef Stew is made the same way; just substitute red wine for the white.

## Ingredients

1 1/2 lbs shoulder of veal
1/4 C flour
1/2 t salt
1/4 t pepper
5 T butter
1 T olive oil
1 onion, chopped
1 clove garlic
1 bay leaf
1/2 C white wine
1 1/2 C chicken broth
1 C tomato sauce
1/2 lb mushrooms
parsley and thyme

## Servings : 6 to 8

# Ucceletti (Veal Birds)

## Ingredients

2 lbs veal scallops, sliced
$1/4$" thick and pounded
thin
salt and pepper
sage
$1/2$ lb prosciutto, cut thin
flour
4T butter
1C dry white wine
$1/2$C hot broth
1 slice Muenster cheese*

## Servings : 6

*Or 2T Parmesan cheese
plus 2T oil

❶ Sprinkle salt and pepper on each slice
of meat; place 2 leaves of sage on each
slice. Cover with prosciutto.

❷ Roll up jelly roll-fashion; secure with
toothpicks or thread. Dust with flour;
shake off excess.

❸ Heat butter in skillet. Over Medium
heat, cook veal birds for approximately
5 minutes until golden brown on
all sides.

❹ Reduce heat; add wine and cook
3 minutes; add broth. Cover; cook
10 minutes longer.

❺ Shake pan to prevent sticking. If
needed, add a little more broth or
wine. Serve immediately with gravy.

Here are 2 other ways of cooking
Uccelletti (Saltimbocca**):

❶ Place a slice of Muenster on sage,
then a slice of ham.

❷ Mix 2T Parmesan cheese plus 2T
olive oil; spread on each slice, then
top with sage and proscuitto.

** Jump into your mouth.

# Braciole

❶ Place oil in saucepan; sauté garlic or onion. Add tomatoes, tomato paste, basil and salt. Simmer.

### Ingredients/Sauce
2T olive oil
2 cloves garlic*
1 lg can tomatoes
1 6-oz can tomato paste
basil
·   $1^{1}/_{2}$t salt

### Servings : 4 to 6

*or 1 onion, chopped, or both

❶ Sprinkle onion salt over meat. Cover meat with oil, cheese and herbs.
❷ Roll each piece from short side; tie with a string. Brown on all sides in oil.
❸ Add meat and drippings to tomato sauce mixture. Simmer until tender, approximately 3 hours.

To tenderize meat before cooking, sprinkle on a little Adolph's (meat tenderizer)before rolling. Don't use salt when you use Adolph's.

### Ingredients/Braciole
$3^{1}/_{4}$" slices top round, approximately 2 lbs
onion salt
2T olive oil
2T Parmesan cheese
parsley, rosemary, thyme
$^{1}/_{2}$t salt
$^{1}/_{8}$t pepper
pinch of sage

# Cutlets (Veal or Pork)

## Ingredients

2 eggs, well-beaten

2 T milk

1/2 t salt

pepper

rosemary, sage or thyme

6 slices veal scallops
or boneless pork,
pounded thin

3 T flour

1 1/2 C bread crumbs

3 T olive oil

3 T butter

## Servings : 6

❶ Beat eggs and milk together; add salt and pepper.

❷ Lightly sprinkle meat with flour on both sides.

❸ Mix bread crumbs with herbs in bowl. Dip each cutlet into egg mixture, then crumbs. Repeat process, dipping each cutlet a second time.

❹ Combine oil and butter in a skillet; heat over Medium until sizzling.

❺ Add cutlets; sauté, browning each side over Low to Medium heat. Cook until tender, approximately 5 minutes per side.

❻ Serve hot with a lemon wedge.

Note: You can stop at this point, or continue as follows:

❼ Stir chopped chives or a chopped onion into 2 T butter; brown. Spoon mixture over cutlets or top each off with 2 T hot tomato sauce.

# Chili con Carne

❶ Cook rice according to package directions.

❷ In frying pan, sauté onion and meat. Sprinkle in flour, salt and pepper; brown.

❸ Add tomatoes, tomato sauce, garlic powder and water. Cover; simmer for 1 hour, stirring occasionally.

❹ Add sugar, vinegar, beans and chili powder; simmer for 10 minutes. Serve over hot rice.

I've always liked chili but Rudy never did—so I always made it when he was away on business trips.

## Ingredients

3C rice

1 ½ lbs chopped meat

1 med onion, chopped

2T flour

1t salt

¼t pepper

1C canned tomatoes

8 oz tomato sauce

1t garlic salt

2½C water

4t chili powder

1t brown sugar

1T vinegar

1 can kidney beans, rinsed

## Servings : 6

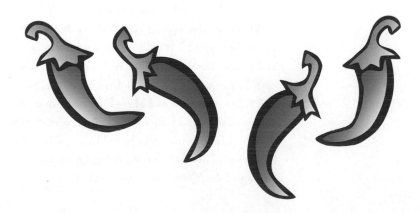

# Mom's Pot Roast

## Ingredients

4 lbs beef eye round

2 bay leaves

1–3 garlic cloves

$^{1}/_{4}$t thyme

2–3 sprigs parsley

salt and pepper

2 onions, chopped

2 celery stalks, chopped

1 carrot, cut into chunks

2C red wine

1C beef broth

1–3T olive oil

2 lg tomatoes

$1^{3}/_{4}$C broth

2 lbs veal bones

4–6 potatoes, quartered

## Servings : 4 to 6

❶ Place meat in non-reactive bowl. Add herbs, onion, celery and carrot. Cover with wine, beef broth and pepper. Cover with plastic wrap; refrigerate for 8–12 hours or overnight, turning once.

❷ Remove beef from bowl; pat dry. Reserve marinade.

❸ In deep pot, heat olive oil; brown meat on all sides.

❹ Add marinade, tomatoes, and additional $1^{3}/_{4}$C broth. Tuck veal bones around meat. Cover tightly; simmer slowly for 4 hours or until a fork easily pierces meat. Add potatoes for last 30 minutes of cooking.

Sometimes I add pearl onions about 20 minutes before the pot roast is finished. Veal bones add flavor but if you can't get them, don't worry. You could also ask your butcher to lard the eye round for you with strips of bacon; in that case, use only 1T of olive oil to brown meat.

There are times when I don't marinate the meat, but rather sprinkle it with Adolph's meat tenderizer and reduce the salt called for in the recipe. In this case, brown meat on all sides, then add wine, broth and tomatoes. At the end of cooking, remove meat and vegetables and keep warm. Add 1T cornstarch dissolved in 2T vinegar to liquid in pot; stir until thickened. This is the gravy; it can be strained (though I don't) and poured over meat.

# Sausage with Peppers and Onions

❶ Cut sausage into 2" pieces. In saucepan, briefly sauté; add salt and pepper.
❷ Add onion, green pepper, parsley and sage to sausage. Sauté until everything is golden brown.
❸ Add wine; cook for 10 minutes.

For a complete meal, I sometimes add diced potatoes to the sausage and cook before adding the onion mix. You could also add mushrooms into the onion mix.

### Ingredients
1 lb luganiga (Italian sweet sausage)
1 lg onion, chopped
1 green pepper, chopped
parsley and sage
2 T olive oil
$\frac{1}{4}$ C red wine

### Servings : 4 to 6

# Chicken Divan

❶ Cut cooked, skinless chicken into long slices.
❷ Cook broccoli until just tender; drain and put in shallow casserole dish.
❸ In top of double boiler set over simmering water, melt butter; stir in flour.
❹ Add broth and milk to butter mixture. Cook, stirring constantly, until thickened. Add salt, pepper and sherry.
❺ Cover broccoli with chicken, then sauce. Sprinkle with cheese. Bake at 400°F for 12 minutes.

I often relied on this recipe to use up leftover chicken and broccoli. You could also use the Cheese Sauce recipe (see p.77) to cover chicken.

### Ingredients
2 large chicken breasts, cooked
1 pkg broccoli spears
2 C water
2 T butter
3 T flour
$1\frac{1}{2}$ C chicken broth
$\frac{1}{2}$ C milk
salt and pepper
2 T sherry
grated Parmesan cheese

### Servings : 4

# Mom's Chicken Pot Pie

## Ingredients/Broth
(this is really Chicken Soup)

2–3 lbs stewing chickens, quartered

1 qt water

3 bay leaves

3 carrots, peeled and quartered

3 med onions, quartered

3 celery stalks

parsley

1t peppercorns

1T salt

¼ lb chopped ham

4 hard-cooked eggs, sliced

### Servings : 8

❶ In large kettle, bring chicken to a boil in salted water.

❷ Add bay leaves, carrots, onions, celery, parsley, salt and peppercorns.

❸ Cover pot; simmer for 30 minutes or until vegetables are crisp-tender. Remove vegetables and chicken from pot; strain broth.

❹ Remove skin from chicken. Cut poultry from bones; cut into chunks.

❺ Put chicken and vegetables in casserole dish.

❻ Add ¼ lb chopped ham and 4 hard-cooked egg slices. Note: This is optional.

❶ In saucepan, melt butter. Stir in flour until smooth, then gradually add broth, pepper, lemon juice, sherry and salt. Cook, stirring, until thickened.

❷ Add 2 egg yolks; stir until thickened. Do not boil.

❸ Pour roux over chicken. Top with Pie Crust (see p.123) or Biscuits (see p.27). With knife, make X-shaped slit in center. Brush top with beaten egg yolk. Bake at 425°F for 30 minutes until golden brown.

This can be simplified a lot by using leftover chicken, frozen vegetables, such as peas and pearl onions, canned chicken broth and packaged pie crust.

## Ingredients/Roux

$^1/_4$C butter

$^1/_4$C flour

2C broth

$^1/_4$t pepper

2T lemon juice

$^1/_3$C sherry

1t salt

3 egg yolks, beaten

# Coq au Vin

## Ingredients

3 1/2 lbs broiler/fryer
    chicken parts
1/4 lb pancetta, diced
1 C broth
1 t salt
1/8 t pepper
8 pearl onions
8 sm mushrooms
1 garlic clove
1/2 C scallions, or
1 onion, chopped
1/8 t thyme
1 bay leaf
2 T flour
2 C red wine

## Servings : 6

❶ In Dutch oven, sauté chicken and pancetta pieces until golden. Sprinkle with salt and pepper.

❷ Add onions, mushrooms, bay leaf, thyme; simmer until golden, approximately 15 minutes.

❸ Add garlic and scallions; sauté for 1 minute.

❹ Stir in flour; slowly add wine. Cook, stirring constantly, until thickened.

❺ Bake chicken and veggies in covered pot for 1 hour at 400°F until tender.

# Breaded Pork Chops
# with Apple Rings

**❶** Sprinkle chops with seasoned flour.
Beat egg with water; dip each chop.

**❷** Roll each in breadcrumbs. Fry in hot
fat or oil until golden and done,
approximately 15 minutes. Add
boiling liquid, then cover and cook
30 minutes until tender.

**❸** Core apples but do not peel. Cut apples
into $\frac{1}{2}$" slices. Melt butter in skillet;
add apples; cook until tender and
lightly browned. Sprinkle 2T sugar
over apples. Serve with pork.

BE SURE PORK IS WELL-COOKED. When
cooked correctly, no pink juice should come out
of chops when pierced with fork.

## Ingredients

8 pork chops, about 2 lbs

seasoned flour

1 egg

breadcrumbs

fat for frying

2T oil

$\frac{1}{3}$C boiling water, broth
or juice

1T water

2 apples

2T butter

2T sugar

## Servings : 3 to 4

# Sauerbraten with Potato Dumplings

## Ingredients/
## Sauerbraten

4 pounds beef eye round

2t salt

1t ginger spice

2 ¹/₂ C water

2C wine vinegar

2 med onions, sliced

2T mixed pickling spice

2 bay leaves

1t whole black pepper

8 whole cloves

fat for frying

¹/₃ C brown sugar

flour

## Servings : 4 to 5

❶ Wipe off meat; rub with salt and ginger and place in bowl. Bring water and all other ingredients except brown sugar to a boil. Pour mixture over meat.

❷ Refrigerate, covered, for 3 days, turning once a day. Remove meat; reserve marinade.

❸ Dry meat with paper towel; brown on all sides in fat or oil in a heavy kettle.

❹ Put on rack in pan; add half the onions, bay leaves and cloves from marinade and 1 cup marinade.

❺ Cover; simmer about 3¹/₂ hours, adding more marinade if needed.

❻ Slice meat. Strain hot marinade; add enough reserved marinade to make 3 cups. Skim off fat; thicken with a little flour, sugar and water. Add meat; serve hot with dumplings.

My friend Emily thickens her gravy with crushed gingersnaps.

❶ Cook potatoes in amounts of salt, water and milk listed.

❷ Beat in flour, eggs and onion.

❸ Shape into 12 balls. Drop into boiling salted water; simmer approximately 10 minutes. Brown crumbs in margarine; sprinkle on dumplings. Any leftover dumplings can be split and browned in margarine.

## Ingredients/Potato Dumplings

2 envelopes instant mashed potatoes

$1^{1}/_{2}$t salt

$1^{1}/_{2}$C boiling water

$^{1}/_{2}$C cold milk

$^{1}/_{2}$C sifted flour

2 eggs

1 sm onion, minced

$^{1}/_{2}$C bread crumbs

$^{1}/_{4}$C melted margarine

# Cassoulet

## Ingredients

1 lb dried red kidney
beans

6C water

1$^1/_2$ lbs pork sausages

1 lb boneless beef chuck,
cubed

2 med onions, chopped

2 cloves garlic, minced

$^1/_2$t dried rosemary,
crushed

2t salt

$^1/_4$t pepper

Pinch cayenne (optional)

$^3/_4$C dry red wine

1$^1/_2$C bean liquid

### Servings : 6

❶ Wash beans. Bring to a boil with 6C
water; boil for 2 minutes. Let stand
for 1 hour, then simmer until almost
tender (or use canned beans).

❷ Cut sausages in half; fry in skillet
until browned; remove sausage.
Brown beef, onion and garlic in fat
remaining in pan; transfer to 3-quart
casserole. Add seasonings and wine.

❸ Cover; bake at 350°F for 1 hour.

❹ Add sausage, beans and bean liquid.
Put cover back on. Bake 1$^1/_2$ hours
longer or until beans and meat are
very tender.

# Corned Beef

❶ Wash brisket; put in large kettle.
Cover it with cold water.
❷ Add pepper, celery, carrots, onion,
bay leaves and vinegar.
❸ Bring to a boil; cover; simmer 4 hours
until tender.
❹ Serve with boiled cabbage and potatoes.

### Ingredients
4 lbs brisket
1 pepper, chopped
1 celery stalk, chopped
1 onion, quartered
2 carrots, chopped
1 T vinegar
2 bay leaves

Servings : 8

# Poached Salmon

❶ In a fish poacher, place onion, celery,
carrot, bay leaf, water and vinegar.
Bring to a simmer. Cover; simmer for
15 minutes.
❷ Place salmon in poacher; sprinkle with
dill, pepper and juices from lemons or
limes. Cover; simmer but do not boil,
for about 10 minutes (depending on
the thickness of the fish).
❸ Drain; serve with lemon or lime wedges,
vegetables and tartar sauce dressing.

**Dressing :** $^1/_2$C mayo or Dijonnaise
(see p.70), parsley, 1t pickle relish,
$^1/_4$t horseradish, $^1/_4$t dill. Blend all
ingredients together. Chill until serving.

### Ingredients
1 onion
1 celery stalk
1 carrot
1 bay leaf
3C water
$^1/_2$C white vinegar
1 lb fresh salmon
dill
pepper
2 lemons or limes

Servings : 2 to 3

# Seafood Medley

## Ingredients

4C cooked, cleaned shrimp

4 7-oz cans tuna

3C cooked lobster or crab

1C French dressing

8C chopped celery

4 peeled, diced cucumbers

$\frac{1}{2}$ C minced onion

1C sliced olives

2t salt

$\frac{1}{2}$t pepper

2 $\frac{1}{2}$ C mayonnaise

3 green or red peppers, slivered

### Servings : 25

❶ Combine seafood in large bowl. Add French dressing; marinate for 1 hour in refrigerator. Drain.

❷ In large bowl, combine fish with vegetables, salt, pepper and mayo. Chill; serve on a bed of lettuce. Garnish as desired with chopped tomato, hard-cooked egg, parsley, etc.

This is great for party buffets.

# Fish with Mushrooms and Wine

❶ Drain mushrooms; reserve liquid. Melt 2T butter in skillet; sauté mushrooms until browned. Remove from skillet.

❷ Roll fish in flour, salt and pepper. Fry in 2T butter and oil on Medium-High heat until brown on both sides, flipping fillets only once. Remove; place on a heated platter.

❸ Put mushrooms back in skillet. Add mushroom liquid; turn heat to High; add wine and 1T butter. Stir 1 minute, then pour over fish. Sprinkle with chopped parsley. Serve with lemon wedges.

## Ingredients

6 oz sliced mushrooms, canned or fresh

5T butter

2 lbs fish fillet (sole, flounder, etc.)

salt and pepper

flour

2T olive oil

½C white wine

parsley

1T butter

### Servings : 4

# Shrimp and Crabmeat au Gratin

## Ingredients

1 pkg frozen artichoke
hearts

$^1/_2$ lb mushrooms

2 T chopped shallots or
onion

garlic

$^1/_2$ T butter

1 lb cooked, cleaned
shrimp

$^2/_3$ C dry white wine

2 cans king crab meat

$^1/_4$ lb butter

$^1/_2$ t pepper

$^1/_4$ C flour

$^3/_4$ C milk

1 8-oz pkg grated Cheddar

2 T bread crumbs

## Servings : 6

❶ Cook artichokes according to package
directions; drain. Sauté mushrooms,
shallots and garlic in butter; add
artichokes.

❷ Add shrimp and wine.

❸ Before adding crab meat, check to see
that all cartilage has been removed.
Mix in crab following directions
on can.

❹ To make cheese sauce, melt butter and
pepper in pan. Take off heat; stir in
flour until smooth. Slowly blend
in milk, then place back on heat and
cook until mixture boils, stirring
constantly.

❺ Add cheese; stir until cheese is melted
and smooth.

❻ Fold shellfish mixture into cheese
sauce. Bake in a buttered casserole at
375°F for 30 minutes. Sprinkle top
with buttered crumbs.

# Risotto e Gamberetti (Rice with Shrimp)

❶ Heat oil and butter in large pot. Add onion; sauté for 5 minutes. Add rice; stir to coat with oil and butter.

❷ Add wine. Heat to boiling until almost evaporated. Add 1C simmering broth; stir until broth is absorbed. Continue to add broth, ½C at a time. Broth should be absorbed before adding more.

❸ Add shrimp, peas and lemon juice with last ½C broth. Cook uncovered, stirring constantly until broth is absorbed, shrimp is pink and rice is tender, approximately 5 to 8 minutes more. Add salt, pepper, and Parmesan cheese. Serve.

## Ingredients

2T olive oil
2T butter
1 onion
1¼C rice
⅓C white wine
4–5C chicken broth, simmering
12oz cleaned shrimp
1C peas
1T lemon juice
½t salt
pepper
parsley
Parmesan cheese

### Servings: 4

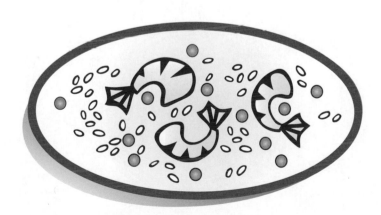

# Stuffed Filets of Sole

## Ingredients

2T butter

2 4$^{1}/_{2}$-oz cans shrimp

1 4-oz can mushrooms

1 lg onion, minced

2T chopped parsley

8 sole filets (3 lbs)

$^{1}/_{2}$t salt

pepper

2 10$^{1}/_{2}$-oz cans condensed
cream of mushroom soup

$^{1}/_{4}$C water

$^{1}/_{3}$C sherry

$^{1}/_{2}$C grated Cheddar

## Servings : 4 to 6

❶ Early in the day: In a skillet, sauté butter, drained shrimp, chopped, drained mushrooms, onion and parsley until onion is soft.

❷ Sprinkle both sides of each fish filet with salt, pepper and desired herbs. On to one end of each fillet, spoon some of the onion mixture, then roll up neatly, fastening with a toothpick. Place fillets in 12" x 8" x 2" baking dish.

❸ In a medium bowl, combine cream of mushroom soup, water and sherry; pour over fillets; sprinkle with grated cheese. Refrigerate.

❹ About 40 minutes before serving: Heat oven to 400°F.

❺ When oven is pre-heated, bake fillets 30 minutes or until they are easily flaked with a fork, but still moist.

# Fried Butterfly Shrimp

❶ Shell raw shrimp; remove black vein. Wash shrimp, cut through back on outside and spread out.

❷ Stir together flour, salt and pepper. Dip shrimp in buttermilk, then flour.

❸ Fry in hot, deep fat (360°F on frying thermometer) until lightly browned. Drain on paper toweling; serve at once. Note: If frozen, reheat in hot oven.

## Ingredients

2 lbs shrimp

1 C flour

1 t salt

$^1/_4$ t pepper

$^1/_2$ C buttermilk

fat for frying

## Servings : 4 to 5

## THOUGHTS ON THANKSGIVING

I give thanks for family; for a husband with
whom to share life's rewards and challenges;
for children and grandchildren; for memories
which are the snapshots of days well spent
and for the anticipation of memories yet to be;
for friendship; for the love in a kiss,
the understanding in a smile; for the miracle of life itself;
for continued good health and for each additional day
which measures out my brief moment in time;
for knowing that there's a divine plan;
for the sunrise and sunset;
the force that stirs the ocean, wind and rain,
and the unseen signal that tells nature when it's time for
its winter sleep and the silent alarm that awakens it each
spring to each day of life.

Inez Ferrari (November 22, 1990)

# Ricotta Pudding

## Ingredients

1 med container Ricotta
cheese
$^1/_4-^1/_3$ C sugar
2 eggs
2t vanilla*
$^1/_2$ C chocolate chips,
regular or mini**

---

## Servings : 6 to 8

*In place of vanilla, you can
use amaretto, rum, etc.
**In place of chocolate chips, you
can use 2T cocoa or 2t coffee.

❶ Beat Ricotta until fluffy. Add sugar, to taste; beat well.

❷ Add eggs; beat well. Add vanilla and chips or cocoa for color, or brewed coffee for flavor. Blend well; chill until served.

This is the easiest dessert, it takes just 10 minutes from start to finish. It's also tasty and nourishing. Big Nonna used to bake it in a ring mold that was buttered and coated with bread crumbs—35 minutes at 350°F—until a knife inserted came out clean. It is sort of like cheesecake, Italian-style.

# Rice Pudding

## Ingredients
1 orange peel
$^1/_2$ C rice
$^1/_2$ C sugar
pinch of salt
1 qt milk, scalded
1 C light cream
2 egg yolks
$^1/_2$ C raisins
$^1/_2$ t vanilla
cinnamon sugar

---

## Servings : 8

❶ Add orange peel, rice, sugar and salt to scalded milk. Cook, covered, over Low heat for approximately 45 minutes.

❷ Remove peel. Mix cream and yolk. Stir small amount of rice mixture into egg mixture, then return this egg/rice mixture back to the pot containing the remainder of the rice. Add raisins; continue cooking, covered, until mixture thickens, approximately 20 minutes. Stir periodically.

❸ Add vanilla; let cool. Chill.

❹ Sprinkle top with cinnamon sugar.

This is a nice, homey winter dessert.

# Baked Caramel Custard
## (Crême Caramel, Latte in Piedi)

❶ Stir sugar constantly over heat until caramelized.

❷ Add warm water slowly; stir until smooth.

❸ Pour mixture into 1-quart ring mold, coating bottom and sides of mold.

### Ingredients/ Caramel

$^2/_3$ C sugar

$^1/_2$ C water

Servings : 8

❶ In bowl, beat eggs, yolks and sugar until blended.

❷ In saucepan, scald milk and cream. Add to egg mixture; flavor with vanilla.

❸ Pour into mold; set in a pan of hot water. Bake at 325°F for 45 minutes. Knife inserted should come out clean.

This is the smoothest, most delicious custard. If you like, it can be made up to two days ahead of time. Be sure to put it into a deep enough dish; caramel will spill out if you don't. Also, loosen around sides before turning out.

### Ingredients/ Custard

4 eggs

4 egg yolks

$^1/_3$ C sugar

1 C heavy cream

$2^1/_2$ C milk

$^1/_2$ t vanilla

# Big Nonna's Lemon Pudding

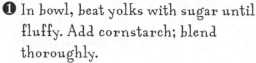

## Ingredients

4 egg yolks

4T sugar

2T cornstarch

2C milk

lemon zest and peel

1t vanilla

liquor-flavored cookies

## Servings : 6

❶ In bowl, beat yolks with sugar until fluffy. Add cornstarch; blend thoroughly.

❷ Scald milk and lemon peel. Slowly add egg mixture to milk, stirring constantly; cook over Low heat until thickened and brought to a boil. Remove from heat.

❸ Cool. Add vanilla.

❹ Line small bowl with liquor-flavored champagne cookies. Pour in pudding. Chill several hours or overnight. Loosen around sides; invert onto a large dish. Serve.

Big Nonna uses Italian lady fingers, which are more like cookies. She dips them in white wine or liquor such as Cointreau. This is one of Rudy's favorite desserts, Big Nonna often makes it for him.

# Big Nonna's Cherry Tart
## (Crostata di Marmelata)

❶ Blend all ingredients together until dough forms. Wrap in plastic; chill 1 hour. If dough is very dry, add up to 2T milk.

❷ Lightly flour work surface; roll out enough dough to cover bottom and sides of greased pie pan. Fill (see below). Use remaining dough to make a lattice work decoration for top of pie. Bake at 450°F for 15 minutes, then at 400°F for 15 minutes until golden brown.

### Ingredients/Pasta Frolla (sweet dough)

2C flour
$^1/_2$ lb melted butter
$^1/_2$C sugar
1t vanilla
1 egg+1 yolk
pinch of salt
2T milk

### Servings : 1 cake

❶ Simmer ingredients, covered, for 1 hour. Uncover; simmer an additional 2 hours until mixture is thick like jam.

This is Big Nonna's favorite tart and Rudy and Gigi really enjoy it, too. She cooks the cherries and makes her own jam; I tried it once but over-cooked the fruit and it became too thick. If you decide to try your own jam, check the consistency every 15 minutes during the final hour of cooking, keeping in mind that it will thicken some as it cools. You can also use any good jam in any flavor to fill the pie crust.

### Ingredients/ Cherry Filling

3 cans sour cherries
1C sugar
1T Kirsch or any flavored liquor

# Chocolate Chip Cake

## Ingredients

¼ lb butter
1 C sugar
2 eggs
2 C flour
1 t baking powder
1 t baking soda
1 t vanilla
½ pkg chocolate chips
1 C sour cream
1 C chopped walnuts (optional)
4 T sugar
2 T cinnamon
melted butter

### Servings : 1 cake

❶ In bowl, cream butter and sugar. Beat in eggs.

❷ On a piece of waxed paper, sift together flour, baking powder and baking soda. Add to creamed mixture. Add sour cream; mix.

❸ Add vanilla, chocolate chips and nuts (if using).

❹ Mix together sugar and cinnamon in small bowl. Pour half of batter into a greased tube pan. Sprinkle with half of cinnamon-sugar mix.

❺ Pour in remaining batter; cover with remaining cinnamon-sugar mix. Add melted butter on top.

❻ Bake at 375°F for 50–55 minutes.

This is another good keeper. My grandchildren love it because of the chocolate chips inside. If I know my grandson Matthew is coming, I make sure to skip the nuts.

# Chocolate Mocha Graham Cracker Pie

❶ In food processor, whirl graham crackers to fine crumbs. (Or, working in batches, place crackers in heavy-duty plastic bag and crush with rolling pin.) Combine melted butter and cracker crumbs. Press mixture into bottom and up sides of a 9" pie pan.

❷ In top of double boiler set over simmering water, melt chocolate chips. Stir in coffee; blend; let cool.

❸ Beat in egg yolks, 1 at a time. Beat egg whites until stiff peaks form, then fold into chocolate mixture.

❹ Whip heavy cream; fold into chocolate mixture. Pour into crust. Refrigerate at least 2 hours before serving.

If you freeze this, it tastes just like ice cream—a chocolate lovers delight! For a crisper crust, bake at 375°F for 6 minutes, then let cool before filling.

### Ingredients
20 graham crackers
3 T melted butter
1 6-oz pkg chocolate chips
1 T instant coffee
3 eggs
1 C heavy cream

### Servings : 1 pie

# Mom's Fabulous Cheese Cake

## Ingredients/Cookie Dough Crust

1 C flour
$^1/_4$ C sugar
$^1/_2$ C butter
1 egg yolk
$^1/_4$ t vanilla

### Servings : 1 cake

❶ In bowl, mix together flour and sugar. Add butter, yolk and vanilla; blend well. Wrap in plastic wrap; chill for 30 minutes.

❷ Lightly flour work surface. Roll out $^1/_3$ of dough to cover bottom of a 9" springform pan. Bake in 400°F oven for 8 minutes or until lightly browned. When pan is cool enough to handle, butter sides; press remaining dough in thin layer all around.

## Ingredients/Filling

1 lb cream cheese
1 C sugar
2 T flour
$^1/_4$ t salt
4 eggs, separated
1 t vanilla
1 C heavy cream

❶ In bowl, cream the cheese until light and fluffy. Add sugar, flour and salt. Blend thoroughly.

❷ Add vanilla and egg yolks; beat well.

❸ Add cream; blend.

❹ Beat egg whites until stiff peaks form; fold into cream cheese mixture. Pour into crust-lined pan.

❺ Bake 5 to 8 minutes at 500°F. Reduce heat to 200°F; bake for 1 hour. Let cake cool in pan for 3 hours. Loosen sides and remove. Chill; top as desired.

After all these years, this is still one of my best cakes. Never mind the calories, it's fabulous! You can top it with cherry or pineapple fillings. Gigi loves this as her birthday cake.

# Pound Cake

❶ Sift flour, baking soda, and $^3/_4$C of
   the sugar into a large bowl. Add
   butter; mix well with fingers.

❷ Add egg yolks, lemon juice and vanilla.
   Mix well with fingers.

❸ In bowl, mix egg whites with salt;
   beat until stiff peaks form. Slowly
   add remaining $^3/_4$C sugar and cream
   of tartar. Beat until thick.

❹ Add egg whites to flour mixture;
   fold in with hands until whites are
   thoroughly incorporated.

❺ Spoon into a greased, floured tube
   pan. Bang pan once on table to remove
   any large air bubbles.

❻ Bake at 325°F for 1 hour. When done,
   cake tester inserted will come out
   clean. Let cool for 15 minutes, then
   turn out onto plate; continue cooling.

This ranks as one of my all-time favorites. I don't
know anyone who didn't like it. Rudy and all the
Grandfathers loved it. It's good plain, with fruit,
dunked in a glass of wine, toasted for breakfast
or for afternoon coffee. It freezes and keeps well.
I always make two, one for the freezer and one
for the moment.

## Ingredients
$1^1/_2$C flour
$^1/_4$t baking soda
$1^1/_2$C sugar
1C butter
5 eggs, separated
$1^1/_2$T lemon juice
$1^1/_2$t vanilla
$^1/_8$t salt
1t cream of tartar

## Servings : 1 cake

# Heavenly Pie

## Ingredients

4 egg whites

2C sugar

$^1/_4$t cream of tartar

1 pkg lemon pie filling

$^1/_2$C heavy cream

strawberries, sliced

---

## Servings : 1 pie

❶ Preheat oven to 275°F. Let egg whites sit at room temp for 30 minutes, then place in large bowl; beat until stiff.

❷ On piece of waxed paper, sift sugar and cream of tartar together. Add slowly to egg whites. Beat continuously until smooth, glossy, stiff peaks form to make meringue.

❸ Line bottom and sides of a well-greased 9" pie pan with mixture; be careful not to get meringue on rim. Bake for 1 hour or until light brown and crisp to the touch. Allow to cool in oven overnight; do not refrigerate.

❹ Make lemon filling according to package directions; cool. Beat heavy cream until fluffy; fold most into lemon pie filling. Top with remaining whipped cream and sliced strawberries.

This one is like a lemon meringue pie, except the crust is made of sugar meringue and you use a lemon-cream filling.

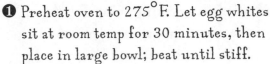

# Lorraine's Carrot Cake

❶ In bowl, combine sugar and oil. Add eggs; beat.

❷ On a piece of waxed paper, sift dry ingredients. Add to creamed mixture; beat well.

❸ Add carrots (or zucchini), vanilla, raisins and chopped walnuts; blend well.

❹ Grease and flour three 8" pans. Bake at 350°F for 45 minutes to 1 hour. Cake tester inserted should come out clean.

## Ingredients

2C sugar

1½C vegetable oil

4 eggs

2C flour

2t baking soda

¼t salt

1t cinnamon

3C grated carrot (or zucchini)

2t vanilla

1C raisins

1C chopped walnuts

### Servings: 1 cake

❶ In bowl, cream butter and cheese. Stir in vanilla. Blend in confectioners' sugar until smooth. Frost.

I first tasted this moist, delicious cake at a Boston museum and have loved it ever since. If you frost it, the cake should be refrigerated because of the cheese and butter in the icing. It's scrumptious, frosted or not. When using zucchini, remove seeds and grate. When Rudy's zucchini would come in, I'd make several cakes and stash layers in the freezer. The credit for this recipe goes to my son-in-law's sister, who so kindly shared it with me.

## Ingredients/Cream Cheese Frosting

¼ lb butter

8 oz cream cheese

2t vanilla

1 lb sifted confectioners' sugar

# Sponge Cake

## Ingredients
8 eggs
1C sugar
1t vanilla
1C flour, sifted

---

## Servings : 1 cake
## (2 to 3 layers)

❶ In bowl, start beating eggs and gradually adding sugar; beat until very thick and pale in color. Stir in vanilla.

❷ Fold in sifted flour until it is no longer visible.

❸ Grease but do not flour 2 or 3 (depending on height of layers desired) 8" pans. Place cut-to-fit waxed paper circles in bottoms of pans; grease.

❹ Bake in a preheated oven at 350°F for 35 minutes or until tester comes out clean.

❺ Cool on rack. Turn out; carefully peel away waxed paper from bottoms. Frost and decorate as desired.

The tricky part of this recipe is folding in the flour so that you don't have little balls in the batter. Try sifting ⅓C of sugar with the flour and beating the other ⅔C with the eggs; it can help. If you still end up with little flour lumps, don't worry; they will fall to the bottom during baking and you can pick them out after the cake has cooled.

This is my all-time favorite sponge cake. I use it for most birthday cakes, Bûche de Nöel, Jellyroll, Strawberry Shortcake and Dobos Torte. It's light and can take any frosting or whipped cream. You can adjust the flavor or color just by adding cocoa to the flour or by varying the flavored extract.

# Dobos Torte

❶ Combine sugar, water and cream of tartar in small pot.

❷ Stir over Low heat until sugar dissolves, then turn heat to Medium-High and boil without stirring until a drop of syrup forms a soft ball when dropped into cold water (238°F on a candy thermometer).

❸ Meanwhile, as syrup cooks, beat egg yolks in bowl until thick and light in color, approximately 3–4 minutes.

❹ Carefully pour syrup into eggs in slow, steady stream. As mixture cools for approximately 10–15 minutes, it should turn into a thick, smooth, cream. Beat in vanilla and cocoa. Then beat in butter, in small pieces, until all absorbed. Refrigerate until used.

❶ In saucepan, mix sugar and water. Boil, without stirring, until sugar dissolves and liquid boils and begins to darken.

❷ Continue to boil until caramel becomes golden brown.

❸ Pour over the top layer of cake. With buttered knife, mark 16 wedges, cutting nearly through the glaze.

## Ingredients/Filling
$1^{1}/_{3}$C sugar
$^{2}/_{3}$C water
$^{1}/_{4}$t cream of tartar
8 egg yolks
2t vanilla
$^{1}/_{2}$C dark, unsweetened cocoa
2C softened butter

## Servings : 1 cake

Note: For the cake, use the Sponge Cake recipe on the previous page. Split each of 3 layers in half, for a total of 6 layers. Fill and frost sides of 5 layers; top 6th layer with the glaze below.

## Ingredients/Glaze
$^{2}/_{3}$C sugar
$^{1}/_{3}$C water

This is a pretty and delicious party cake. Nicole and Michelle would ask for this on their birthdays. Brush a little rum or liquor on the cake layers before frosting. Work quickly when scoring the glazed layer.

# Mocha Buttercream Frosting

## Ingredients

1 C sugar
$^1/_3$ C water
$^1/_4$ t cream of tartar
4 yolks, well-beaten
5 oz semi-sweet chocolate
$^1/_4$ C brewed coffee
$1^1/_2$ C butter
2 T rum

## Servings : 4 cups

❶ Combine sugar, water and cream of tartar in small pan. Bring to a boil; stir only until sugar dissolves.

❷ Boil rapidly until syrup spins a long thread.

❸ Gradually beat syrup into the beaten, light, fluffy yolks; continue beating until thickened.

❹ In top of double boiler set over simmering water, melt chocolate in coffee. Stir into egg mixture.

❺ Beat in butter, a few tablespoons at a time. Stir in rum. Chill until appropriate spreading consistency.

Buttercream frosting, my favorite, takes a little time to make but it's worth the effort; the result is smooth, creamy and not as sugary as other frostings. You can color or flavor it as you wish. I like it with sponge cake. Press chopped nuts on the sides of your frosted cake, or dribble cooled melted chocolate over the top. Decorate with fancy tips or shaved chocolate. Be creative!

# Seven Layer Cake

❶ In bowl, beat egg yolks until thickened and lemon-colored. Add sugar gradually, beating constantly with rotary beater; add 1 T lemon juice.

❷ On piece of waxed paper, sift together dry ingredients. Add in batches, alternating with remaining lemon juice and beating until smooth. Beat egg whites until stiff peaks form; fold into batter.

❸ Grease but do not flour 2 or 3 (depending on height of layers desired) 8" pans. Place cut-to-fit waxed paper circles in bottoms of pans; grease. Spread a few tablespoonfuls of batter in each.

❹ Bake in very hot oven, 450°F, about 5 minutes or until lightly browned. Turn out on racks to cool; carefully remove waxed paper. Repeat process until all batter is used and 7 layers are baked. Frost between layers, top and sides with Butter Cream Frosting (see p. 120).

## Ingredients

6 eggs, separated
1 1/4 C sugar
2 T lemon juice
3/4 C sifted flour
1/4 C cornstarch
1/2 t salt

Servings : 1 cake

# Lady Finger Mousse Cake

## Ingredients

3 squares unsweetened
baker's chocolate
$^1/_2$C sugar
salt
$^1/_4$C hot water
1T cold water
$1^1/_2$t granulated gelatin
4 egg yolks
1t vanilla
4 egg whites, stiffly beaten
$^1/_2$C heavy cream, whipped
2 dozen lady fingers

---

## Servings: 1 cake
## (8 to 10)

This is a wonderfully
impressive refrigerator cake
that I made quite often when
we were expecting
company. It can be made up to
three days ahead and frozen,
covered with plastic wrap.
I liked to dip the lady fingers
in a little rum, Amaretto, or
Frangelico as an added touch.
If desired, add $^1/_2$C finely-
chopped, toasted walnuts to
chocolate mixture before
turning into mold.

❶ In top of double boiler set over
simmering water, melt chocolate.
Add sugar, dash of salt and hot water,
stirring until sugar is dissolved and
mixture is blended.
❷ In small bowl, add cold water to
gelatin; stir. Add gelatin mixture to
hot chocolate mixture; stir until
gelatin is dissolved. Cook until
mixture is smooth and well-thickened.
❸ Take off heat. Add egg yolks one at a
time, beating thoroughly after each
addition. Place back atop water; cook
2 minutes, stirring constantly. Add
vanilla; let cool.
❹ Fold mixture into egg whites; chill.
Fold in whipped cream.
❺ Line bottom and sides of mold with
waxed paper. Arrange lady fingers on
bottom and sides. Add thin layer of
thickened chocolate mixture. Continue
to add lady fingers and chocolate
mixture in alternating layers, ending
with chocolate mixture. Cut off excess
lady fingers around top; arrange cut
pieces on chocolate mixture.
❻ Chill 12 to 24 hours in refrigerator.
Unmold.

# Mom's Apple Pie

❶ Put flour, salt and baking powder in large bowl.

❷ Cut in shortening with pastry blender or two butter knives until mixture forms pea-sized balls. Add water; blend until dough holds together.

❸ Wrap in plastic; chill for 30 minutes.

❹ For an open-faced pie: Divide chilled dough in half. Place one part between 2 floured, waxed paper sheets. Roll out from center to a circle 2" larger than pie pan; gently press into pan and up sides. Prick dough with fork; line with foil. Bake at 450°F for 10 minutes; remove foil; cool. Add cooked filling (see p. 124). Continue to bake at 325°F for 30 minutes.

❺ For a closed-faced pie: Divide chilled dough in half. Place one part between 2 floured, waxed paper sheets. Roll out from center to a circle 2" larger than pie pan; gently press into pan and up sides. Prick dough with fork; line with foil. Bake at 450°F for 10 minutes; remove foil; cool. Meanwhile, roll out other half of dough into slightly smaller circle for top crust. Add cooked filling, see below, to bottom crust. Lay top crust in position; crimp edge all around. Brush with egg wash, then prick with fork. Bake at 425°F for 40–45 minutes.

## Ingredients/Pie Crust

3C flour
$\frac{1}{2}$t baking powder
$\frac{1}{2}$t salt
1C shortening
$\frac{1}{2}$C cold water
egg wash (1 yolk+1T water)

## Servings:
1 closed-face pie

# Mom's Apple Pie (cont.)

### Ingredients/Filling
2T butter

³/₄C sugar

1T lemon juice

6–8 apples, peeled, cored, quartered and sliced

2T flour

2T cold water

1t cinnamon

❶ In large frying pan, melt butter, sugar and lemon. Add apples; stir to coat; simmer for 10 minutes. Remove apples; place in pie crust.

❷ In bowl, dissolve flour in water. Add a little hot syrup to flour-water mixture; stir well. Add this back into the hot syrup, stirring constantly until syrup thickens.

❸ Pour syrup over apples; sprinkle with cinnamon.

Every fall, we'd trek to a farm in upstate New York for apples. My favorites are Granny Smiths, Cortlands and Rome Beauties. To make a crumb topping for an open-faced pie: Mix together ³/₄C brown sugar, ¹/₂C flour and ¹/₄C butter.

# Little Nonna's Pasta Frolla Cookies

### Ingredients
4T butter

³/₄C sugar

2 eggs

1t vanilla

1¹/₂C flour

2t baking powder

### Servings : 2 dozen

❶ In bowl, blend butter and sugar. Add eggs and vanilla. Blend in flour and baking powder until dough forms.

❷ Shape dough into "S"-shaped cookies. Place on greased tray or fit into a greased pan.

❸ Bake at 375°F for 30 minutes or until golden.

Little Nonna made these cookies for Rudy, he really loved them.

# Key Lime Pie

❶ In bowl, combine crumbs and butter.
Press into bottom and up sides of 9" pie
pan. To smooth, position another 9"
pie pan on top; press down.

❷ Crust should be in place when second
pan is lifted. Refrigerate until filled.

### Ingredients/Crust
6 oz (³/₄C) finely-crushed
graham crackers
6T melted butter

### Servings: 1 pie

❶ In bowl, beat yolks until very thick,
approximately 4-5 minutes.

❷ Beat in condensed milk and lime juice.

❸ Pour mixture into pie crust; refrigerate
at least 4 hours or until filling is firm
to the touch.

❹ Before serving, top with cream that
has been whipped with 1T sugar.

You can bake this crust for crispness if you like.
Just add 4T sugar to pie crust mixture; bake at
375°F for 8 minutes. Let cool before filling.

### Ingredients/Filling
6 egg yolks
1C key lime juice
2 cans 14-oz sweet
condensed milk
1C heavy cream, whipped

# Posy Cream

❶ In bowl, cream shortening and butter.
Add confectioners' sugar and vanilla;
beat until smooth. Put into pastry bag;
use tips to form flowers, leaves, etc.

### Ingredients
1C shortening
¹/₄C butter, softened
3C sifted confectioners'
sugar
1¹/₂t vanilla

# Buttercream Frosting

### Ingredients
<sup></sup>1/3 C butter
1/8 t salt
3 C sifted confectioners'
sugar
1/8 C light cream
1 1/2 t vanilla

❶ In bowl, cream butter, salt and 1 C confectioners' sugar until fluffy.

❷ Add remaining sugar, light cream and vanilla. Beat until smooth.

# Ornamental Frosting

### Ingredients
2 1-lb pkgs confectioners'
sugar
1 t cream of tartar
6 egg whites
1 t vanilla

❶ Sift sugar and cream of tartar into large bowl.

❷ Add egg whites; beat. Add vanilla; beat until so stiff that a knife drawn through mixture leaves a clean path.

❸ Divide into glasses. Tint with food coloring as desired; mix well. Put into pastry bags and use for decorating, then let dry.

❹ If making Christmas tree ladies (see p. 140) make more green than red or blue. While frosting is still soft, you can add sprinkles, etc.

# Cream Puffs and Éclairs

❶ Preheat oven to 375°F. In saucepan, bring water, butter and salt to boil. Turn heat to Low. Immediately add flour all at once; with wooden spoon, begin beating mixture. Beat until mixture leaves sides of pan and forms a compact ball. Take off heat; continue beating for approximately 2 minutes.

❷ Add eggs, one at a time, beating well after each addition until mixture is thick again. After adding the last egg, beat until mixture has a satin-like sheen.

❸ Drop rounded tablespoons of dough about 6" apart in rows that are 2" apart on ungreased baking sheet. For éclairs: Shape each ball of dough into a 4"x1" rectangle, then round sides and pile dough on top. For cream puffs: leave round.

❹ Bake about 45 minutes or until golden and puffed. Remove from oven; immediately cut small slit in center of side of each with point of knife. Bake another 10 minutes to be sure interior is cooked. Remove; let cool on rack.

❺ Split on 3 sides, then fill. Top with chocolate glaze; refrigerate until filled.

## Ingredients/Pastry

1 C boiling water
½ C butter
¼ t salt
1 C sifted flour
4 eggs

———

## Servings : 16

# Cream Puffs and Éclairs (cont.)

## Ingredients/Filling

1C milk
1t vanilla
3 egg yolks
¼C sugar
2T flour or 1T cornstarch
2T butter

❶ Pour milk into 1-quart pan; scald. Add vanilla. Take off heat.

❷ Beat yolks in bowl. Add sugar and flour. (Flour thickens with a heavier consistency than cornstarch but either can be used). Beat until well-blended.

❸ Whisk half of milk into eggs until blended. Pour egg mixture into pan with balance of milk; blend again.

❹ Return pan to Medium-Low heat. Cook, stirring constantly until mixture comes to a boil and thickens, approximately 1–2 minutes. Continue stirring until smooth and thick, approximately 1 minute.

❺ Take off heat. Stir in butter until melted and blended. Push cream through sieve into bowl.

❻ Cover surface of cream with plastic wrap. Poke 6 to 8 slits in plastic with tip of knife to allow steam to escape, which prevents skin to form on top. Chill for up to 3 days.

❼ Fill éclairs or creampuffs with a spoon or pastry bag fitted with an extra-large writing tip. If you prefer, you can use whipped cream.

❶ In top of double boiler set over simmering water, mix chocolate, butter and water until melted. Take off heat; stir in sugar. Spoon over filled éclairs or creampuffs; let set.

### Ingredients/ Chocolate Glaze

2 T butter

2 squares unsweetened chocolate

4 T hot water

$1^{1}/_{2}$ C sifted confectioners' sugar

# Crêpes Suzette

❶ On piece of waxed paper, sift flour. Sift flour again with sugar and salt. Combine eggs, milk, butter and lemon rind in separate bowl. Gradually stir egg mixture into flour mixture until smooth.

❷ Heat small skillet, greased lightly with butter, over Medium heat. Pour about 2 T batter into skillet; quickly tilt to spread into thin layer. Cook until set and browned; turn; brown other side.

❸ Grease skillet again if necessary. As each crepe is cooked, place on a shallow pan or cookie tray, roll. Cover with clean towel to keep warm until ready to serve.

### Ingredients/Crepes

$^{1}/_{2}$ C flour

1 T sugar

$^{1}/_{8}$ t salt

2 eggs, well-beaten

$^{2}/_{3}$ C milk

1 T butter, melted

$^{1}/_{4}$ t grated lemon rind

### Servings : 4 to 6

# Crêpes Suzette (cont.)

## Ingredients/Suzette Sauce

6T butter
3T sugar
$1/4$t grated lemon rind
$1^1/_2$t orange rind
$1/_3$C orange juice
3T brandy (optional)

❶ Melt butter in 10" skillet. Add sugar, lemon and orange rinds and juice. Stir over Low heat for 5 minutes. Add crêpes, one at a time, unrolling to coat with sauce. Re-roll while still in skillet using two forks.

❷ Serve warm in orange sauce. Or, sprinkle with brandy, carefully ignite and spoon flaming sauce over crêpes.

# Crumiri Cookie

## Ingredients

$1^1/_2$ sticks+2T butter
$3/_4$C sugar
2 eggs
$1^3/_4$C flour
salt
$2/_3$C+1T cornmeal

Servings:
Approximately 2 dozen

❶ In bowl, cream butter and sugar until light and fluffy.

❷ Add eggs; blend well.

❸ On a piece of waxed paper, sift flour, salt and cornmeal together. Blend into creamed mixture.

❹ Roll small pieces of dough $1/_2$" thick. Place on greased, floured cookie sheet. Bake 12 minutes at 325°F until golden.

# Christmas Delights

# Bûche de Noël

❶ Make sponge cake batter. Pour batter into jellyroll pan that has been greased, lined with waxed paper and greased again. Smooth top of batter.

❷ Bake at 375°F for 15–20 minutes or until done when cake tester inserted comes out clean.

❸ Turn out onto a dish towel that has been sprinkled with confectioners' sugar. Peel off waxed paper. Cut off crusts on all 4 sides, then roll tightly, using towel to help, starting from longer edge of cake layer. You will end up with a long, cylindrical jellyroll shape.

❹ Wrap in towel; let it rest and cool.

❺ Unfurl; fill with chocolate or mocha buttercream frosting. Re-roll; place on tray. Position small pieces of waxed paper around edges so that tray does not get messy while you apply frosting to log.

❻ Decorate with meringue mushrooms shaved chocolate, etc. so finished cake looks like a tree log.

## Ingredients

Sponge Cake recipe
(See p.118)

Mocha Butter Cream
Frosting (See p.120)

Meringue Mushrooms
(See p.132)

### Servings : 1 cake

This is our pretty Christmas cake. It's log-shaped (bûche) and meant to symbolize the traditional Yule log. Delicious; all our grandchildren say it's "beeootiful"!

# Meringue Mushrooms

## Ingredients

4 egg whites

$^1/_4$t cream of tartar

$^1/_8$t salt

1t vanilla

1C sugar

$^1/_2$C chocolate chips

cocoa

---

## Servings : 30 cookies

❶ Preheat oven to 225°F. Line 2 cookie sheets with foil.

❷ In bowl, beat egg whites, cream of tartar and salt at High speed until soft peaks form. Slowly add sugar, 2T at a time, and vanilla. Beat until sugar dissolves and stiff peaks form, approximately 5 minutes.

❸ For Stems: Fit pastry bag with plain tip. Spoon meringue into bag; it's easier to fill if you first stand bag in a tall jar. Shape stems by holding bag straight up against cookie sheet; use small knife to cut meringue from tip. Make stems about 1$^1/_2$" long. Make more stems than caps because some stems will topple during baking.

❹ For Caps: Use remaining meringue in bag. Shape by holding tip close to foil; hold bag vertically and press to form a small mound. Smooth with finger dipped in water. Place this tray on bottom rack of oven; place tray with stems on top rack. Bake for 1 hour at 225°F. Turn oven off; let mushrooms cool in oven with door slightly open until dry.

❺ In top of double boiler set over simmering water, melt chocolate chips. With knife, spread underside of cap with chocolate, or, dip flat side of stem into chocolate. Place stem onto cap; let dry. Store at room temperature in lightly- covered container; do not freeze. Mushroom tops may be dusted with cocoa.

These cookies are so pretty and melt in your mouth. I would decorate my Bûche de Nöel with a few. It's time-consuming but well worth the effort. It's a good way to use up extra egg whites, too.

# Russian Kisses

❶ Preheat oven to 400°F. In bowl, cream butter and ½C sugar until light and fluffy. Add water and vanilla; blend. Add flour and pecans. Beat until well-mixed. Wrap in plastic; chill 30 minutes or until firm.

❷ Roll into 1" balls. Place on ungreased cookie sheet 1" apart. Bake for 10 minutes or until light brown on bottom.

❸ Let cool for 10 minutes, then roll in remaining 1C confectioners' sugar. When completely cool, roll in sugar again.

Another good keeper; they look like little snowballs.

## Ingredients

1C butter
1½C confectioners' sugar
1T water
1t vanilla
2¼C flour
¾C chopped pecans

## Servings: 4 dozen

# Butterfly Cookies

### Ingredients
1 C butter, chilled
1 1/2 C flour
1/2 C sour cream
3/4 C sugar

**Servings : 40 cookies**

❶ In large bowl, cut butter into flour with a pastry blender or two butter knives, until mixture resembles coarse crumbs.

❷ Stir in sour cream until well-blended.

❸ Place dough on waxed paper; shape into a 4" square. Wrap in plastic; refrigerate for 2 hours.

❹ Unwrap dough; cut into 4 equal pieces. Work with 1 piece at a time while keeping others in the refrigerator.

❺ Sprinkle 2 T sugar on waxed paper. Coat all sides of dough with sugar. Roll out into a 12"x5" rectangle.

❻ On a 12" edge, lightly mark center with tip of knife. From each 5" edge, roll dough towards center line, jelly-roll fashion. Wrap well in waxed paper; chill in freezer for 20 minutes.

❼ Repeat Step 6 with the remaining pieces of dough.

❽ Preheat oven to 375°F. Line two cookie sheets with foil. Place 1/4 C sugar on waxed paper. Cut each roll into 1/2" slices. Dip each side in sugar; place on baking sheet 2 1/2" apart. Bake for 15 minutes until golden around edges. Turn with spatula; bake 5 minutes more. Remove immediately.

These are crisp and flaky, and are among my favorites. I can never seem to make enough; they disappear in no time. Yummmmmm!

# Lace Cookies

❶ Melt butter in medium-sized pan.
Add flour, sugar, oatmeal and cream
all at once. Cook, stirring constantly,
just until mix starts to bubble. Take
off heat. Stir briskly for a few seconds.

❷ Drop rounded teaspoonfuls about 4"
apart onto well-greased, lightly-
floured cookie sheet. Bake only 5 to 6
cookies at a time, at 375°F for 5-6
minutes or until golden.

❸ Let cool for 2 minutes on baking
sheet, then remove carefully with
spatula and drape over rolling pin
until firm. If cookies harden before
they can be removed, reheat a few
seconds to soften again.

This is a fragile, crisp cookie. The tricky part
is taking them off the sheet and putting on the
rolling pin or cardboard paper towel core. You
can also make them smaller and leave them flat;
just lift and place on closed brown paper bag;
then you can dribble melted chocolate chips over
them. Either way, they're delicious.

## Ingredients

$^1/_2$ C melted butter
$^1/_4$ C flour
$^1/_2$ C sugar
$^3/_4$ C quick cooking oatmeal
2 T light cream

**Servings : 2$^1/_2$ dozen**

# Hang-Yen-Bang
## (Chinese Christmas Cookies)

### Ingredients

2¹/₂C flour

³/₄C sugar

¹/₄t salt

1t baking powder

³/₄C butter

1 egg+1 yolk

1t vanilla or almond
extract

3T water

¹/₃C almonds

---

### Servings : 3 dozen

❶ On piece of waxed paper, sift flour, sugar, salt and baking powder together. In bowl, beat butter and 1 egg together until creamy. Add extract, almonds and 2T water; blend.

❷ Gradually add flour mixture to butter mixture. Stir until blended and a dough that comes away from sides of bowl is formed. On lightly floured work surface, knead until smooth. Wrap in plastic; chill 1 hour. Preheat oven to 350°F.

❸ From dough, form 1" balls. Place on greased cookie sheet ¹/₂" apart. Press an almond into center of each. Mix 1 yolk and 1T water together; brush mixture over cookies. Bake at 350°F for 25 minutes or until golden.

These are Rudy's favorite at Christmas. I always make a double batch because they don't last long. The cookies keep well and can be frozen, too.

# Spitzbuben

❶ In bowl, cream butter and sugar. Add vanilla; blend.

❷ Add almonds and flour; blend well or knead, if you wish.

❸ On a floured board, roll dough to $\frac{1}{8}$" thickness. Cut with simple cutters such as hearts or diamonds. Place on ungreased cookie sheet. Bake at 350°F for 20 minutes or until lightly browned.

❹ While cookies are still hot, dip one side of each half into bowl of granulated sugar. Spread jam on one side of cookie; top it with matching shape to form sandwich.

These keep well when stored in a covered tin. These are one of our all-time favorite Christmas cookies, and have become Gigi's special Christmas project.

## Ingredients

1C+3T soft butter

1C sugar

1t vanilla

2C ground almonds

2C flour*

1 jar seedless black raspberry jam

## Servings : 5 dozen

*You may have to add or take away some flour, depending on consistency of dough.

# French Dip/Butter Nut Cookies

## Ingredients

2 C flour

$^{1}/_{4}$ C sugar

$^{1}/_{2}$ t salt

1 C butter

2 t vanilla

extras such as chopped nuts, sprinkles, jam, cinnamon

## Servings : 3 dozen

❶ In large bowl, sift flour, salt and sugar.

❷ Add butter and vanilla; blend well.

❸ Shape into balls, logs, or crescent shapes. Bake on ungreased cookie sheet at 325°F for 25 minutes.

❹ For Frenh Dips: Dip baked cookies into melted chocolate chips, then sprinkles.

For Butter Nut Cookies: Roll raw dough balls into 1 beaten egg white, roll in chopped nuts, then bake.

For Sweeties: Roll baked cookies in confectioners' sugar or roll unbaked dough balls in cinnamon-sugar before placing in oven.

For Criss-Cross Cookies: Prior to baking, flatten dough balls with fork in one direction, then the other, to form criss-cross pattern.

For Jam Cookies: Prior to baking, poke pinkie finger in center of dough ball, fill with a tiny bit of jam, then bake.

This cookie is crisp, buttery and versatile. Look at all the different results you can get with one recipe. I know that you'll come up with other ways to decorate them. They can be frozen or stored in a tightly-lidded cookie tin. These are one of my Christmas or anytime cookies.

# Gingerbread Men

❶ On piece of waxed paper, sift together
flour, soda, ginger, cinnamon and
salt together.

❷ In bowl, cream shortening with
brown sugar until light and fluffy.
Add egg and molasses; mix well.

❸ Gradually add flour mixture; beat
well. Wrap dough in plastic; chill
dough 1–2 hours.

❹ On floured work surface, roll out
dough to ⅛" thickness. Cut into
gingerbread men shapes, my pattern
measures 5⅛" x 3½". Place on
greased cookie sheet.

❺ Bake at 350°F for 12 minutes. If
using for tree ornaments, pierce holes
In tops with skewer. Let cool; decorate
with Ornamental Frosting (see p. 126).

You can also use raisins, pieces of cherries or
gumdrops for decorating. These little cookies
always adorned our Christmas tree. When my
daughters were younger, they'd all get in on the
act, each decorating her own. It was a lot of fun!

## Ingredients
2½C flour
1t baking soda
½t salt
1t cinnamon
1t ginger
½C shortening
¾C brown sugar
1 egg
½C molasses

## Servings : 60 cookies

# Christmas Tree Ladies
## (Old-Fashioned Sugar Cookies)

### Ingredients
$^2/_3$C butter
$1^1/_2$C sugar
2 eggs
1t vanilla
4C flour
$2^1/_2$t baking powder
$^1/_2$t salt
4t milk
cream, a beaten egg white
or a beaten egg yolk
diluted with water

### Servings : 6 dozen

❶ In bowl, beat butter and sugar until blended. Add eggs and vanilla; blend until very light and fluffy.

❷ On a piece of waxed paper, sift together flour, baking powder and salt. Add to butter mixture; blend. Add milk; blend. Wrap in plastic; chill until dough is easy to handle, approximately 2 hours. Or, place in freezer to hasten chilling.

❸ On a lightly-floured work surface, roll out half of dough to $^1/_8$" thickness; cut out shapes. Place cookies $^1/_2$" apart on greased cookie sheet. Brush with cream, a beaten egg white, or an egg yolk diluted with water.

❹ Bake at 400°F for 9 minutes or until light brown. If using for ornaments, pierce holes in tops with skewer. Let cool.

❺ To the left is the Christmas Tree Lady example, but you can use your own patterns if you like. My pattern measures $5^1/_8$" x $4^1/_4$". I use sprinkles and Ornamental Frosting (see p.126) to decorate these cookies, plus melted chocolate chips for "hair." These cookies, along with Gingerbread people, have been my family's traditional Christmas tree decorations. They're gladly pulled off the tree for any little one who comes to visit.

# Linzertorte

❶ In bowl, cream butter. Gradually beat in sugar until light and fluffy.

❷ Beat in egg yolks one at a time. Add vanilla; stir well.

❸ On piece of waxed paper, sift together flour and baking powder; fold into butter mixture. Fold in ground nuts.

❹ Pour batter into greased, floured 9" springform pan. Bake at 350°F for 45–55 minutes or until done.

❺ Let cool. There will be some shrinkage. Dust top with confectioners' sugar.

This is one of my holiday cakes. It freezes well, so it can be made weeks ahead of time. I always make extras for gift giving. My brother, Nando, likes this one very much. There's another version that tops the cake with raspberry jam.

## Ingredients
1⅓ C butter

1¼ C sugar

6 egg yolks

1t vanilla

2⅓ C flour

1t baking powder

1 C unblanched almonds, ground

2T confectioners' sugar

## Servings:
## 1 cake (12 to 16)

# Little Nonna's Holiday Recipes

These three recipes are my mother's, who got them from her mother. Christmas just wouldn't be the same without them. I wish Little Nonna could know what a hit her cakes are!

## Spongata (Mama's Christmas Fruitcake)

### Ingredients/ Pasta Frolla

$^1/_4$ lb butter

1 C sugar

3 eggs

2 t lemon flavoring

3 C flour

$^1/_2$ t baking powder

---

### Servings : 1 cake

❶ In bowl, cream butter and sugar. Add eggs and flavoring; stir well.

❷ Blend in flour and baking powder to form a soft dough. Wrap in plastic; chill for 30 minutes.

❸ Split dough in half. Roll out each to fit 10" pie, making one slightly smaller for top, between 2 pieces of floured wax paper.

❹ Grease 10" pie pan; place larger circle in pan. Add filling, see below. Position smaller circle on top; crimp edge all around. Pierce top crust with fork.

❺ Bake at 275°F for 1 hour. Halfway through baking, gently press down on top crust to help it adhere to filling. When done, a knife inserted should come out clean.

❶ In bowl, place raisins with enough white wine to cover; let soak for 1 hour.

❷ In bowl, beat butter with sugar, honey, mostarda syrup and egg yolks. Add cinnamon, nutmeg, vanilla, orange flavor and brandy; mix. Add drained raisins and nuts; mix.

❸ Fold in stiffly-beaten egg whites.

Rudy and my son-in-law, Lorrin, love this cake.

## Ingredients/Filling

1 C raisins

white wine

¹/₄ lb melted butter

1 C sugar

3 T honey

3 T mostarda syrup

2 eggs, separated

¹/₄ t cinnamon

¹/₄ t nutmeg

1 t vanilla

1 t orange flavor

3 jiggers of brandy

¹/₂ C pignoli

2 C chopped walnuts

1 C chopped hazelnuts, pecans or peanuts

# Little Nonna's Walnut Cake

## Ingredients/Pasta Frolla

2 egg yolks

2 C flour

1 ¼ C butter

1 t vanilla

½ C sugar

½ t lemon zest

### Servings : 1 cake

❶ Sift together dry ingredients into bowl. Add remaining ingredients; knead into a dough. Wrap in plastic; chill.

❷ On floured work surface, roll out dough, reserving a small piece, to fit 10" pie pan. Position in pan. Roll remaining dough into strips for top.

❸ Add filling, see below; arrange dough strips on top. Bake at 375°F for 45 minutes to 1 hour.

## Ingredients/Walnut Filling

2 lb bag chopped walnuts

½ C sugar

¼ lb butter

3 T liquor, such as amaretto

2 T rum

1 lemon rind, grated

❶ Whirl walnuts in blender or work bowl of food processor to chop finely. Place walnuts in bowl; add remaining ingredients; mix into a paste.

This is my brother's favorite Christmas cake.

# Little Nonna's Ricotta Pie

❶ In bowl, cream Ricotta until fluffy. Add sugar, eggs, rum and vanilla; stir.

❷ Make same pie crust as for Little Nonna's Walnut Cake (see p. 144). The only difference is that this cake has a top and bottom crust. Don't forget to prick top crust to keep it from puffing up.

❸ Fill pie crust; bake at 375°F for 45 minutes to 1 hour or until filling is set and a knife inserted in center comes out clean.

This pie is like Italian cheesecake.

## Ingredients/Ricotta Filling

1$\frac{1}{2}$ lbs Ricotta cheese

$\frac{1}{2}$C sugar

3 eggs

3T rum

1t vanilla

### Servings : 1 cake

# Index